E. HAANEL CASSIDY
PHOTOGRAPHS 1933-1945

E. HAANEL CASSIDY PHOTOGRAPHS 1933-1945

MAIA-MARI SUTNIK

With a foreword by Ruth Bains Hartmann

OCTOBER 3 - DECEMBER 6, 1981

ART GALLERY OF ONTARIO/MUSÉE DES BEAUX-ARTS DE L'ONTARIO

TORONTO/CANADA

The Art Gallery of Ontario is funded by the Province of Ontario, the Ministry
of Culture and Recreation, the Municipality of Metropolitan Toronto, and the
Government of Canada through the National Museums Corporation and the
Canada Council.

Design: Paul Haslip
Duotones: Coach House Press
Printing: Proving Specialties Ltd.
Typesetting: Trigraph

Frontispiece:
No. 40. *Plant Form – Potentials*; Hawaii, 1938
Chloro bromide
35.1 × 25.7 cm
On the cover:
No. 9. *Paradise Regained*; Japan, c. 1935-36
Silver bromide
24.8 × 29.9 cm

Canadian Cataloguing in Publication Data
Sutnik, Maia-Mari
   E. Haanel Cassidy: photographs 1933-1945

Catalogue of an exhibition held at the Art Gallery of Ontario, Toronto, Oct.
3-Dec. 6, 1981.
Bibliography: p.
ISBN 0-919876-75-7

1. Photography, Artistic—Exhibitions. 2. Cassidy, E. Haanel—Exhibitions.
I. Cassidy, E. Haanel. II. Art Gallery of Ontario. III. Title.
TR647.C37 1981   779′.092′4   C81-094923-7

CONTENTS

PREFACE

In 1938 Martin Baldwin, Curator of the Art Gallery of Toronto, now the Art Gallery of Ontario, organized an exhibition of E. Haanel Cassidy's photographs. It was the twenty-sixth exhibition at the Gallery devoted to photography since 1917.

While often cited as lacking in response to the medium, the Art Gallery of Ontario has in fact through its exhibition program been involved with photographs, and continues to be involved in the belief that the medium is a significant image-making process practised by artists of diverse personal visions. This exhibition of Cassidy's photographs serves both as a posthumous honour to an independent and little known Canadian photographer, and as a study of his photographs in relationship to the prevailing trends in photography. Although the influences of pictorialism and what is known as "the straight aesthetic of photography" (as distinct from the more subjective manipulated image), discussed in the essay provided by Maia-Mari Sutnik, are present in Cassidy's work, his overall expression was dedicated to personal concepts of beauty in nature and its relationship to higher universal principles of harmony and unity. This philosophy motivated Cassidy to undertake intense investigations of his environment. These personal statements are expressed in a number of series and sequences of photographs.

We hope this exhibition will reinstate the appreciation demonstrated by Dr. Baldwin, and that Cassidy's black-and-white photography will become better known, perhaps to exceed the reputation he achieved as a leading colour photographer for Condé Nast in New York during the 1940s and 1950s. We are most grateful to Mr. Joshua M. Gitomer for lending from his collection generously, and to the Historical Library, Nevada City, California, for their part in its preservation. We are also grateful to Ruth Bains Hartmann for providing the introductory essay and appreciate the loans made by her and her husband, Erich Hartmann, to this exhibition.

WILLIAM J. WITHROW,
Director,
Art Gallery of Ontario

ACKNOWLEDGEMENTS

When Joshua Gitomer in 1979 proposed an exhibition of Eugene Haanel Cassidy photographs, Cassidy himself was vitally active, working toward completion of the text for his book on gardening. In my conversation with him in January 1980, he was very much looking forward to his reunion with the Art Gallery of Ontario and Toronto, the city he had left almost forty years ago. He was to provide for this catalogue an essay about his life and the documentation for his photographs, which had been rescued by Mr. Gitomer. The impression I had was of a highly articulate and forthright person – the kind one senses has read much and seen much. One felt immediately that experiences and vicissitudes had left emphatic marks on a thoughtful and spirited mind that communicated deeply felt values with more than academic effect. Cassidy died suddenly on April 16, 1980, at the age of seventy-seven.

The reconstruction of such an extraordinary life, so esoteric and intricate in philosophical sources, as well as the growth of Cassidy's philosophy and its influence on his photographs and his life, are things that cannot be done easily. No doubt Cassidy's own descriptions of the events surrounding his photography would have been vastly more penetrating.

I am extremely grateful to both Ruth and Erich Hartmann for giving of their insight, and for providing me with various accounts of Cassidy, making the man and the photographer more accessible. I am also grateful to Joshua Gitomer for overseeing the project and for giving access to Cassidy's negatives, essays, and private papers. The assistance of Sylvia Matthew, Cassidy's daughter, now living in Edinburgh, Scotland, has been invaluable. Both she and Shivani Lucki of Ananda community provided the outline for the chronology. The detailed and demanding task of cataloguing the photographs was expertly done by David Harris, an advanced student in the history of photography at The Courtauld Institute of Arts, London, England. Elaine Tolmach of The Montreal Museum of Fine Arts and Diana Edkins of Condé Nast, have given their time generously for research and information.

Members of the staff of the Art Gallery of Ontario have collaborated in many capacities; Karen McKenzie, Head Librarian, Larry Pfaff, Reference Librarian, Eva Robinson, Registrar, Kathy Wladyka, Assistant Registrar, Barry Simpson, Exhibition Coordinator, Denise Bukowski, Head of Publications and Design, Faye Craig, Assistant to the Coordinator/Photographic Services, Larry Ostrom, Head Photographer, Ed Zukowski, Conservator, Ralph Ingelton, Practitioner/Conservation, Ches Taylor, Technical Services, and his preparations staff, and particularily Marilyn Jacobs, who prepared the manuscript for the catalogue. Special acknowledgement is due to Katherine Lochnan, Curator of Prints and Drawings, not only for her valuable counsel and for sharing my enthusiasm for photography, but for her vision and commitment to development of an exhibition program for photography in its many diverse forms of artistic expression.

MMS

A PERSONAL REMINISCENCE

Haanel Cassidy was a friend. It was a friendship sometimes difficult and demanding, but one that continued through the last thirty years of his life. When my husband Erich and I first met him he was a leading photographer with Condé Nast in New York, where he lived in a small walk-up flat that was piled high with books and with magazines in which his work had appeared. The untidiness on the floor was totally out of keeping with the spectacular display of meticulously tended house plants in and around the windows. Our visits to this magazine-filled conservatory were not unlike sessions with a respected university department head–eccentricities were almost flaunted, tedious anecdotes repeated and I, young and newly married, felt as if I were being tested and usually found wanting. Cups of very strong coffee, ritually ground and prepared from his own selection and blend of coffee beans, were served with an accompanying lecture on the unworthiness of all other blends and methods of preparation, and there was usually a show of photographs. He showed us only his black-and-white photographs–many of them in this exhibition–never his current commercial work, which he dismissed with a characteristic finger-shaking wave of the hand as "selling his soul."

He was a slim, agile man who seemed much taller than he was because of his always-erect bearing and impeccable tailoring. His voice was deep and resonant and rumbled forth in a hearty infectious thunderstorm of laughter that doubled him over with delight, particularly if the joke were of a verbal, punning type.

As years passed and our children were born, our relationship with Haanel softened. He became less of a photographic mentor to my husband and more of a friend of the family. He took delight in children and always enjoyed the company of our son and daughter. By this time he was living in a little house on an estate north of New York City, where his gift for gardening fashioned a paradise of flowers and greenery. He was generous and patient with advice and cuttings but firm about methods of cultivation.

Occasionally he spoke of Japan, where he was born of Canadian Methodist missionary parents, where he returned to teach after his marriage, and where his children were born. He responded to the rigorous discipline of Japanese life and art and he deplored the efforts of missionaries to change an ancient civilization. One can imagine how well suited he was to his earliest profession as schoolmaster in a Japanese boys' school–a person of unquestioned authority in a setting where that authority was respected in every way. One oft-repeated recollection was of his bowing servant bringing tea on a little bamboo tray, the cup always placed just so and the arrival timed exactly. The story comes easily to mind because the little tray now sits on our hall table. The traditions of the Japanese tea ceremony and of flower-arranging appealed to his almost feudal ideas of behaviour, and it is easy to understand why his first photographs taken in that milieu, assumed the form they did. As he became increasingly aware of the dangers inherent in the growing militarism in Japan, he fled the country with his family shortly before World War II.

He talked with us about his own photography, about his

techniques which, arising as they did from his own aesthetic, produced pictures different from prevailing trends in the profession. Indeed, it would be fair to say that he found most other photography inferior. It was bound to be, in his view, because it proceeded from a faulty and inferior philosophy, from a materialism that he despised and from a "humanism" that he regarded as the cause of that materialism. This attitude was somewhat difficult to understand, and further explanation was not forthcoming. Such discussion was usually closed with the observation that the shortcomings of most other photography should be obvious and, if they were not, then it was because of one's own faulty philosophy and insufficient study. He felt that his photographic aesthetic was not recognized and acclaimed in the profession and, because it was not, he abandoned his personal photography. The pictures in this exhibition, his major black-and-white work, were made more than thirty-five years ago. After about 1945 his photographic work was almost wholly in colour.

When his guardianship and financial responsibilities for his children – who were at school in England – were fulfilled, he resolved to end his photographic employment. He would go somewhere to "hermetize," to use his word, and to continue his meditations and studies. He disposed of his belongings, bought special gear, and travelled on a freighter to southern Chile, after having earlier reconnoitered and rejected Lima as a possibility. He took with him farming equipment, some books, a typewriter, and a battery-operated music system, but only at my husband's urging did he take a camera – on loan. He later told us that he never used it.

For years thereafter we kept in touch by letter – through his Chilean stay, which collapsed as a combined result of bad weather and bad choice of location, and through two different ventures in southern California, until his settling in the Ananda community in the Sierra Mountains. His letters described his way of life, his difficulties with extremes of weather, and his gardening, which had expanded from house plants to flowers to vegetables. We also exchanged reading recommendations; he was a faithful reader of *The New Yorker* and the Book Section of the *New York Sunday Times*, to both of which publications he subscribed from whatever far shore he inhabited.

After his departure for Chile in the early sixties we saw

him only three more times. Twice in the early seventies he visited us in New York on his way to see his children in Scotland and in Canada, and we had talks far into the night about his meditations and studies and about the realm of the spirit.

He had chosen to follow an Indian master who had died years before Haanel's arrival at the Ananda community. In the zeal of his beliefs – even as his missionary parents (whose efforts he had always decried) had yearned to spread Christianity – he wanted desperately to convert us, to show us his true way, not only because he knew it was right, but because he loved us. I disappointed him by rejecting the authoritarianism and the preoccupation with self that his philosophy entailed. Yet, in spite of our inability to become disciples, I believe he enjoyed the two visits with us. He revelled in the attention (he was endearingly susceptible to flattery) and the service, after years of living alone. He listened hungrily to

Figure 1. Cassidy with Ruth Hartmann at the Ananda community in California in the late 1970s. (E. Hartmann, © Magnum.)

our records and seemed to enjoy everything, from the late Beethoven Quartets to the Noël Coward songs. As he left, he urged us to visit him in Ananda, to see where and how he lived, telling us lugubriously that we must come "before it was too late." Indeed I wanted to go, to see how he had resolved his life, what his surroundings were, and whether his chosen way was bringing him contentment.

About a year before his death we did visit him, making the long journey from San José, where work had taken us, up into the Sierra Mountains, where he lived in somewhat scruffy solitude in a small geodesic dome in the Ananda community. It was a beautiful place – a robin on the very top of a pine tree sang to the first rays of the sun and soft-eyed deer watched us in the morning silence as we went from our forest hut down to Haanel's for breakfast. He had chosen from the beginning to live in "The Retreat," a place set aside for those in private meditation, and he remained essentially apart from community affairs, with one notable and important exception. His legacy to Ananda is that he passed on to willing and patient disciples his expert and carefully thought-out knowledge of gardening. His monument, in addition to a few photographs, is his creation in a hostile environment (hot dry summers, wet muddy springs, inferior soil) of a garden that flourished. Here, as with his photography, and with everything else that he attempted to teach, it was his philosophy that had to be followed. His rules for gardening and for photography were rigid and were rooted firmly in his own aesthetic.

He was an enigma – a fascinating set of contradictions. A doctrinaire vegetarian who made his own bread and eschewed sugar and refined flours, he was all his adult life a heavy smoker of unfiltered cigarettes and he drank large quantities of strong and bitter coffee. He lived as a hermit in a commune. Although he always spoke against missionaries, he was disappointed that his children and we, his long-time friends, would not be converted to his philosophy. He was a diligent searcher for the true path to God. Although earthly serenity eluded him, on the way and in the search he created and left some evocative photographs and a growing garden.

Ruth Bains Hartmann
June, 1981

A PHOTOGRAPHIC VISION

A STATEMENT OF BEAUTY

Eugene Haanel Cassidy's Photographs from 1933-1945 arc a collection of images which reveal very private inspirations for realizing beauty. Cassidy's vision – deeply rooted in the conviction that art belongs to the realm of the ideal, an ideal inherent not only in nature, but in what nature might be – was never meant as representation. Central to his images is the concept that we are to see them as an indelible link between a substance of beauty and a higher spiritual reality, through which he perceived the world. For a period in his life, black-and-white photography provided the measure of transcendence that imparted to Cassidy inner unity and harmony with the universe and its mysteries.

No other medium has had such a preoccupation with statements of beauty, and perhaps no medium is as well equipped to bring forth beauty as cogently as photography. Except in those situations where the camera becomes simply a device for recording an event, or for presenting the transitory, photography from its beginnings impelled beauty. The earliest photographic images on paper were called "calotype" – derived from the Greek work *kalos*, meaning beauty – and the mirror images of the daguerreotype were not only radiant, but encased as precious objects.

Mid-nineteenth-century photographers went in search of images as trustworthy observers – to provide photographic statements of authenticity and veracity, the "realism" that the medium was capable of. But the scenic wonders, the architectural monuments, and the exploration of new territorial frontiers gave way to freer interpretation of the world. Photographers were constantly in search of competitive and striking images, but their arrested surface realities never told the truth – the camera was not inclined to tell the truth – and since no two photographs of the same object could be indentical, the medium soon gave way to personal evaluation and free expression. Photography would before the end of the century be championed as a medium for works of art.

Some photographers adopted the aesthetic values of genre painting, and others were inspired by Impressionism. Nature, perceived by many as being synonymous with Truth and Beauty, also provided the photographers with intense experiences of creative expression. By the turn of the century, the single-mindedness of some photographers had marked photography as a personal exploration, an effort to embody the beautiful through carefully selected subjects and formal qualities of technique and style. Alfred Stieglitz's legendary *Camera Work* between the years 1903-1917 upheld images embellished by fine reproduction technique. The images in each issue were beautifully composed and placed, and were realized in a format appropriate to such statements of beauty. The perception of the world as beautiful in its detail was most forcefully advanced in Albert Renger-Patzsch's *Die Welt ist Schön* (The World is Beautiful) in 1928. Through the most commonplace objects, seen by the camera in isolated surroundings, fragments, and close-ups, photographers made the audacious statement that by seeing "differently"–more photographically–by experiencing the forms and shapes that eyes would not normally apprehend, the world promised to be a more beautiful place. The Bauhaus artists guided their vision by the beauty found in pure form; industrial machinery, technological instruments, and the scientific phenomena of the world in microcosm were all to reveal the beauty of natural and man-made objects through photography. László Moholy-Nagy's *The New Vision: From Material to Architecture* (1928) and Andreas Feininger's *The Anatomy of Nature* (1956) and *Forms of Nature and Life* (1966) have become exemplary models of the search for beauty by the stunning effects of framing, dazzling light patterns, and bold abstract designs.

The most relevant visions of beauty have held positions that see the world not only through pleasing forms, but invariably through a "new way" of seeing beauty, one that challenges existing notions. Ward Muir's exhibition in Britain, *The Facts of Beauty* (1919) indicated that beauty could only reside in unaltered photographic facts. Edward Weston's terms of reference for a "stark beauty that a lens can so exactly render" became more metaphorical and illusionary than stark, as natural forms of dunes and peppers appeared like many variations on the female form, in itself a classical prototype for beauty. Not surprisingly, photography's historical models for statements of beauty are also reflected in the popular desire to take unencumbered images of nothing more than that which serves the memory as beautiful. Conversely, there is an equal desire to look attractive for the camera; photographs of fashion trends are always more beautiful and alluring than real life.

While notions of beauty are being challenged and questioned in photography because the world in fact has disorder and chaos, photojournalism has attempted to supply the missing sense of veracity with captions and descriptive text to explicate the images. Photographs of the bizarre, the grotesque, and violent scenes of war tell us of all the things that are not beautiful, but these images of suffering, anguish, and devastation receive the most reluctant acceptance as works of art. Too frequently seen as mass communication directed toward individual conscience, these photographic images outlast the relevance of their content, become distanced, and are

seen more for their graphic forcefulness. When chosen as art, they are selected more for their paradoxical or surrealistic content, as usually seen in painting, collage, and other visual forms. The cross-section of the American population in Robert Frank's seminal *The Americans* (1959) at once seen critically as twisted and biased is, however, presented in Jack Kerouac's introductory words as brimming with "agility, mystery, genius, sadness and strange secrecy" and as indescribable "in its beautiful visual entirety." The remarkable images of Garry WinnograND's *Public Relations* (1977), and Lee Friedlander's *The American Monument* (1976), disparate and without any notions of beauty, augment the telling juxtapositions of chance and ephemera with a kind of sheer beauty in photographic virtuosity; they are intuitive and rapid responses to and descriptions of time and place.

Photography's canons for beauty have been ambiguous,

Figure 2. Cassidy in his New York City apartment in 1949. (Photo: Erich Hartmann.)

even disturbing, but beauty has endured as a philosophical basis, and today it is as intrinsic to many photographers' work as it has been in the past. While one cannot draw the conclusion that photography's greatest strength lies in its remarkable pursuit of beauty, unquestionably the medium has spurred the belief in using the camera as a sensitory and metamorphosing instrument that can reveal the hidden structure of all things and permit us to discover an existence of a large universe. While such spiritual precepts have not been unique to photography, the attraction of the camera is its capacity for altering time into preserved instants. This fixing of time, this enduring stillness, is what contributes largely to the great authority of the beauty that can be seen in photography.

Eugene Haanel Cassidy's philosophy of art, the philosophy he practised in his vision as a photographer, is best summarized by a statement he made in 1949, four years after he had all but given up his personal work:

Great works of art are born from the union in something approaching perfect balance of profound inspiration and masterly technique. While inspiration is unquestionably primary, the two are mutually dependent and interact upon each other with an inextricably subtle rhythm. The heat and the force of inspiration sweep technique to transcend itself, and unforeseen nuances revealed through the response of technique push inspiration forward to explore new frontiers of insight. Thus the uninhibited interplay of the two brings forth a creation of beauty neither inherent nor foreseeable in either. This new beauty which has come to birth, this real creation, exists neither in the one or in the other, nor even in both together, but in and around and above the two.

JAPAN

In 1930 Cassidy returned to Japan for the first time since his childhood. He had recently married, graduated from the University of British Columbia, and won The H.R. MacMillan Scholarship, which provided funds for travel.[1] After a brief stay in Tokyo (his birthplace), he secured a teaching position at a boy's school in the town of Yamagata. There he took up photography first using a plate camera.[2] It would be speculative to try to determine the inspiration for this sudden interest in photography. It may have been partly Cassidy's inquisitive mind and partly his strong visual sense that found an outlet in taking pictures.[3] Nor was it very unusual for Westerners spending time in foreign cultures to turn to photography as a part-time hobby for recording the spectrum of traditions. The notion that the medium served reality, preserving memory of the past and at the same time capturing the present, held enormous appeal for travellers. For Cassidy, however, the camera became more than a means of capturing sights and impressions vividly and quickly. It became an inspiration to master its unique capabilities, technically and aesthetically.

Photography in Japan, after a slow beginning, began to flourish in the late 1850s, when the country opened up widely to Western culture and technology. Most early photography reflected foreign taste for the exotic and had little, if any, aspiration to art.[4] Photography also experienced prejudice as a "missionary art" and as an instrument to be feared.[5] By the late nineteenth century the medium, while not esteemed, was extremely popular. Government organizations for the industry, initially slack, began to acknowledge the insufficiency by sending photographers, technicians, and scientists to Europe to be educated in the field.[6] By 1930 advances in trade and production had taken great strides, and a variety of photographic societies were established. Just as the development of the photographic industry had relied on imports from the West, so had aesthetic inspirations. In the 1931 edition of *Photograms of the Year*, Shinzo Fukuhara summarizes the prevailing trend in art photography:

Progress in the photographic matters in Japan has been steady and successful since last report. . . . During the latter half of 1930 two successful exhibitions were held in Tokyo respectively by the Tikyo Shashin Kenkyukai and the Niho Kogwa Kejohi. The former included both tehnical and pictorial works of great interest. The Naniwa Club also held their nineteenth exhibition at Isaka. This was very successful. Another interesting effort was that of the International Tourist Bureau of the Imperial Railway. Photographs of distinctive scenery of the picturesque islands of the Empire were invited and they were all titled "The Autumn of Japan." The result was so satisfactory that the same project is being repeated for the "Winter," "Spring," and "Summer" of Japan. In the spring. . . the Japanese Photographic Society's seventh exhibition was held. This dealt both with the practical and theoretical side of photography. . . The largest exhibition of the current year was the Fifth International Salon of Tokyo. . . . This is an international exhibition that has prospered with friendly support from foreign countries. . . it is said the exhibition reached the total of 3,722 prints. . . the activity of the Japanese photographers continues unabated. [7]

Paralleling the driving force of the salons and the camera clubs were other emerging influences of European art – cubism, surrealism, constructivism. The mass influence of pictorialism, the Bauhaus ideas of a new unity through art forms, *Neue Sachlichkeit* (New Objectivity) and, "other trends from the West, meshed with the cultural tradition of Zen and the theory of *satori* – [the concept that] knowledge comes from successive waves of *illumination*, effected by the interaction of subjective impressions and intuitions with facts and objective elements"[8] – makes rationalization of the varied influences on photographic concepts a difficult task. Placed in the Japanese visual tradition, these Western ideas characterized much of Japanese photographic practice and were accountable for images of ambiguity, innovation, simplicity of design, and remarkable beauty. In the late 1920s a national photographic epoch was in its genesis, but at the same time the wide range of influences also contributed to confusion, and to the tendency toward a norm that had become mere artifice, romanticized and sentimental. [9] Raycen Narusawa wrote in the 1932 *Japan Photographic Annual*:

Disillusioned by the age of imitative pictorial photography patterned after paintings which was in vogue until recently and which lasted for some years, most of our photographers. . . have had their eyes opened to the truth that their pictorial works should be absolutely photographic. . . . Thus, the works of present-day pictorialists must be, to win merit, expressed through the medium of the camera. In this connection. . . our pictorialists are now trying to meet the technical and aesthetic limits of photography. . . they are finding a way out of old limits that Japan's "artistic photography" confined them to. [10]

Cassidy, as an aspiring photographer living in a remote area in the north, was largely isolated from these diverse developments, both by geography and by the difficulty of learning from handbooks and manuals on photography. While not conclusive, it can be assumed that he obtained instructive literature from Britain, and Kodak publications from the United States. [11] Such self-instructive lessons usually contained the necessary technical processes and frequently asserted theories on aesthetic expression that relied on "solutions" for achievement of pictorial ideals. Often handbooks illustrated the results of techniques that alluded "truth" and "beauty" and "artistic effect." It seems evident that Cassidy in his zeal to master techniques would have observed all ideas that came his way, that pictorial values appealed in part to his investigations. His aesthetic persuasions can also be attributed to his contemplative nature and to the character of the man; placing value on his inner resources and on overcoming obstacles and on the freedom to discover means of expression as a personal exploration of one's philosophical and aesthetic intent. Once Cassidy had mastered technique – working long hours in a makeshift darkroom that he had constructed under a staircase in his dwelling[12] – his solutions to photography seemed to him completely original, workable, and uncomplicated by any prevailing fashions.

His early investigations and experiments were to formulate the basic concepts seen in Cassidy's personal work throughout the years. Many years later, he wrote:

In his search for that type of truth known as aesthetic truth, the photographer is bound by the qualities and characteristics and by the limitations of his medium, and since that medium happens to be one of the most rigidly defined and limited, it is one of the most difficult. It is difficult enough technically, but the real difficulty lies in bending that technique away from mere recording, from literal realism, toward an aesthetic expression of individual vision. [13]

None of Cassidy's first experiments with the plate camera have survived. The earliest existing photographs in this exhibition are a Whistler-influenced, *Prows* (No. 1), a veiled landscape *Evening Calm* (No. 5) and a shimmering *Temple Morning* (No. 6), addressing values embodying beauty through choice of subject matter, harmonious compositional arrangements, diffused focus, modulation of tone, and textured surface quality. Such concepts have their origin in late nineteenth-century pictorialist tradition, which advocated photography as a fine art. Cassidy's development exhibited many identical objectives. The pictorialists repudiated images that served as mere aid to memory, as records, or as bare documentation of scientific appearance; the view of the purpose of photography was felt lacking in meaning to human experience and therefore, artistically inhibiting in its emphasis on machine-like "perfection." The duality of photographic technology and personal expression in the medium became a most controversial issue.[14] Ever since H.P. Robinson (1830-1901) in his far-reaching *Pictorial Effects in Photography* published in 1869, elevated subject matter by exhortation towards the very picturesque and painterly genre compositions, the issue of art versus science gained further momentum through varying discourses on aesthetic values and aims. Peter Henry Emerson (1856-1936), a spokesman for a "naturalistic" vision, openly attacked Robinson's practice of elaborate combinations of negatives aimed toward achieving synthetic effects of illusion and decoration. Emerson challenged popular conventions with his basic premise that the nature of the photographic medium existed in its own right, and proceeded to provide new technical approaches and a new aesthetic concept: "the imitation of the effects of nature on the eye."[15] He introduced differential or "naturalistic" focussing, finding his support in Hermann von Helmholtz's theory of physiological principles that the human eye was not constant–it relied on sharp or clear central vision and marginally experienced an "appearance" or impression. The rivalry between the degree of focus–soft and blurred or sharp and salient–and the underlying issue of the relationship of photography to nature predominated as a central debate.[16] This division in the aesthetics of "pure" and pictorial photography has been a key issue in attempts to substantiate a "proper" identification of the medium.

Collectively, pictorialism lost some of its attraction after World War I. Influential groups such as the Linked Ring in Britain, and The Photo-Secessionists in the United States had dissolved. But declarations for pictorialism continued in a variety of paths–through camera clubs, professional and amateur associations, and the international salons. In Japan during the thirties, soft-focus and manipulated imagery were still impor-

tant role models in photography, as well as formalist *avant-garde* images from Germany and the plea for straight photography as called for by Narusawa. The late popularity of pictorialism in Japan was partly due to the belated establishment of a united photographic front–a number of photographic groups had banded together earlier, but it was not until 1927 that the First International Photographic Salon was held in Tokyo and Osaka[17]–and, notably due to the part pictorialism played in its identification with beauty in nature, to which Far Eastern concepts of art readily assimilated.

Japan offered Cassidy a special place for his frame of mind to develop. He had much admiration for the conventions of the country's social relationship, its adherence to discipline, and a respect for Japanese Zen philosophy.[18] Zen reinforced Cassidy in evoking a complete universe and intensifying the natural tendency to seek the essential and the immediate in art through sober and simple means; and in the conviction "that harmony is the main requirement...and the aesthetic ideal is one of a restrained and melancholic beauty."[19] For Cassidy, the view

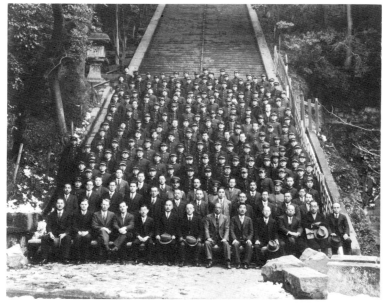

Figure 3. Cassidy (third from left) with faculty and students of the boys' secondary school at which he taught in Shizuoka, Japan, in the mid-1930s.

that Japanese "painters use a few pen-strokes to suggest an area of emotion; their concern is not the explicit description of reality but the evocation of a particular mood, the description of an emotive atmosphere"[20] held easy affinity. Years later he wrote:

Art communicates emotion, but not raw emotion. . . . Art abhors the particular; it must generalize – of course from the particular – but always away from the particular towards the universal. In so doing it adds a mysterious element to aesthetic emotion which is quite distinct from the emotion arising from direct experience (however difficult this special element may be to define).[21]

Cassidy, particularly sensitive to Japan's artistic tradition, admired their calligraphy and avidly collected various kinds of handmade paper.[22] The land and the culture offered an environment that was not at odds with his own developing sense of a higher reality of beauty and abstraction. In his notes he says:

As an example of mastering abstraction, it is instructive to observe a Japanese painter in action. In the pure Japanese tradition at least, he never paints from life. He will take a walk through nature and no one can observe more totally than he – every leaf, every twig, every pebble. Then he will return to his studio, lay the materials to receive the painting (unsized silk or paper) on the floor, and sit and gaze at it until he sees what he wants. Finally with one swift and totally controlled movement he will brush in the curve he imagined.[23]

The methodology of Japan's artistic traditions was influential on Cassidy's approach to his own work. He also drew his inspiration from observation of nature and the countryside. Since only very few of Cassidy's photographs taken in Japan have survived, it is difficult to establish precisely where he photographed and if any contacts were made with other photographers. In 1933 he was living in Shizuoka, teaching again at a secondary boys' school. The town was a short distance south of Tokyo and would have provided him with the possibility of being in touch with the burgeoning photographic activity. The same year he bought the new standard Exacta camera[24] which had just been manufactured by Ihagee in Germany. The camera, a compact single-reflex, using rollfilm (VP 127 – 4 × 6.5 cm negative) offered decisive advantages for ground-glass framing of each exposure.

Cassidy set about to photograph the lush landscape around Shizuoka, to capture its elements of beauty at different times of the day.[25] These early works are soft and lyrical interpretations relying on blurred focus (Nos. 3, 4). The negatives were manipulated in development for their tightly controlled tonal range[26] and enlarged to meet Cassidy's requirement for a "fine print," which appeared in its final form on mat textured paper. During this period of experimentation he would occasionally shift to close-up views of blades of grass, branches, and flowers. Very few of his close-up prints from this period exist, but the surviving negatives reveal that these stylized and restrained compositions drew inspirations from *Ikebana*, the Japanese art of flower arrangement. Later, the faces of Japan began to interest Cassidy, and he would photograph people in their activity or as he encountered them on the road (Nos. 10 and 11).

While there is some sentimentality and awkardness in the treatment of these subjects, Cassidy interpreted with more clarity and definition, and seemed aware that more precision was appropriate for the desired results. His negatives reveal him to have been frequently dissatisfied with the film frame; he cropped radically, designing for a more intimate study of the subjects for his final print. Cassidy felt the photographer was:

not so often confronted by a blank space which he is free to fill piecemeal, but seeks and finds his compositions as a regular practice by segments of physical reality within his searching frame. . . . it should make him "edge conscious" as it were. . . . Awareness of the frame and its bounded space as an active organizing agent produces a sense of a more strongly individualized microcosm than response to gravity and balance alone could ever do.[27]

In order to balance subject matter, he was not averse to completely altering the original image by painting out on the photograph, as the figure of a boy behind the rock in *Paradise Regained* (No. 9); this compositional remedy is barely discernible.

After a few years of taking photographs, Cassidy no longer saw himself as an amateur, but as a professional photographer. He undertook commissions for commercial portraits in Tokyo. His personal work he organized into sets with numbered sequences for viewing. For the most part they were carefully monogrammed or signed, and titled poetically, and some bear more matter-of-fact descriptions of the subject. During this period a great many of his photographs carry a stamp of reproduction protection, clearly suggesting that he saw his work as suitable for reproduction and exhibition. To further emphasize that the photograph "must in itself be a thing of physical beauty"[28] Cassidy determined careful placement of the print and chose special mounts. (The condition of these prints is now poor and they are no longer suitable for exhibition.) He also submitted his photographs to international salons; traces of exhibition stickers indicate that his work received acceptance.

Shortly before leaving Japan in 1937, Cassidy once again turned to landscape. He had avoided photographing the natural wonder of Mt. Fuji, because he found the number of commercial and exploitive images of it appalling.[29] However, his resistance faltered and as a last gesture he made a series of highly composed views, of which four are included here (Nos. 17-20). His treatment, a return to softer focus, emphasized expressive qualities of light, as well as framing for a strong spatial relationship between the foreground and the evanescent mountain in the distance. As a final but pithy statement to indicate his outrage at nature defiled, he photographed the mountain with a spewing smoke stack, ironically titling it *Incense* (No. 18).

By the time he left Japan, Cassidy had found in photography not only a medium to master through technique, but one that could best articulate his beliefs in a pictorial mode through emphasis on the individual's spiritual and artistic philosophy. In many ways, photography served as a testimony to Cassidy's perception of the unfolding of his own spiritual nature, an inward search for underlying universal principles that incorporated truth and harmony through self-realization and heightened perception that transcended the physical world. Cassidy declared:

The principles of aesthetics must be firmly rooted in the nature of the cosmos as any rules of ethics, and cannot be altered or abandoned by personal whim.[30]

Although it may have begun for Cassidy as an act of whim, photography had become more of an act of faith on which to pattern his aesthetic and philosophy. The fact that his visual ideas and concepts in 1937 were not in agreement with the consensus of opinion made no impression on Cassidy whatsoever. He dismissed the influence of pictorialism as only an historic benchmark; "straight" photography was mere documentation; colour was an attempt at verisimilitude and false realism.[31] He felt his own theoretical constructs of a higher vision and purpose were expressed by dignity and beauty in photography. To him, technical control of the camera, abstraction through rendering of tone scale, manipulation of the print, and aesthetic truth offered the proper impulses for the medium.

HAWAII

During the spring of 1938 Cassidy and his family left Japan, returning to Canada by way of Hawaii. Very little information has come to light about the brief time he spent there. It is believed he exhibited his photographs,[32] but this has not been fully established. The record shows, however, that Cassidy had an extremely prolific period of photography. He discovered in many native plants, trees, and flowers a new subject to explore. The forceful natural patterns and designs and the wealth of detail in surface structure, provided Cassidy with a new way of investigating close-up views. Of the Hawaiian series about sixty negatives have survived to reveal the intense scrutiny of photographic abstraction.

This type of investigation was not new to photography. As early as 1914 Charles Sheeler (1883-1965) and Paul Strand (1890-1976) in 1915 had approached subjects with extreme close-up views. Strand was among the first to advocate a re-orientation in photographic aesthetics to "straight" photographic methods.[33] Both Alfred Stieglitz and Edward Steichen (1879-1973) abandoned their earlier pictorial mode of manipulated images and set out to master a purer technique.[34]

Edward Weston (1886-1958) also repudiated his earlier pictorial statements and began a re-examination of his work. Along with a number of photographers he formed Group f.64 in 1932. (The name refers to a lens setting of small aperture to achieve detailed rendition.) Their purpose was to perfect the technical as well as the philosophical aspects of the straight approach. Weston expressed this philosophy in his *Daybooks*:

To see the *Thing Itself* is essential: the quintessence revealed direct without the fog of impression...
Significant presentation, – not interpretation.
My way of working –
I start with no preconceived idea –
discovery excites me to focus –
then rediscovery through the lens –
final form of presentation seen on ground glass, the finished print previsioned complete in every detail of texture, movement, proportion, *before exposure* –
the shutter's release automatically and finally fixes my conception, allowing no after manipulation – [35]

This stress on objectivity, a kind of new realism, was simultaneously taking place among the German *avant garde*. *Neue Sachlichkeit*, a term first applied in 1924 to denote a group of painters who rejected expressionism in favour of neo-realist style, indicated a new realism. [36] In photography this path was characterized best by the work of Albert Renger-Patzsch (1897-1966); he accentuated beauty and design in natural and manufactured objects.

The new attitude toward a purer purpose of the camera, stressing its qualities of precision, and its authenticity as a recording instrument were identified by Cassidy, but only insofar that such elements were part of the "ambiguity of photography itself" [37] he felt that a mixture of science, skill, and vision of the subject matter determined the approach, and the photographer's role was one of discernment.

The Hawaiian photographs have a strong resemblance to the new objectivity and the straight aesthetic. Cassidy, however, was highly circumspect about any presentation that would categorize his work in light of other aesthetics, and he stated in his chapter on photographic truth:

All these predominantly scientific and factual images are to photography-as-art very much what the terms of the laboratory and science textbooks are to the poet... the artist-cum-camera must be constantly on his guard against the more scientific powers of his instrument... as artist he must consistently resist being bullied into seeing as his camera sees... rather force it to accept his point of view,

to see and record what he sees as he sees it. Only so can he achieve images... psychologically sound and aesthetically true. [38]

As if to further reiterate that there was no visible relationship between his close-ups and those adhering to straight interpretation, he states:

With certain types of subjects abstraction can be achieved through the correct choice of focus. For the photographer focus is not by any means a matter of getting everything sharp. He must not only get exactly the right place in sharpest focus, but... to exactly to the right degree... with other types of subjects abstraction can be accomplished through the right exposure and development. Large segments of the tone scale can be dropped by this means. [39]

The essential difference was not only an attitude towards subject, but also artistic resolution. For Cassidy, "previsualization" of exposure was simply a knowledge of the desired end result. It was unimportant whether the subject was free of manipulation or not, what was important was to hold a contemplative position that would express beauty of form, emotion, deepening of insight, and "broadening of contact with the universe," [40] to be seen in the final print.

For Cassidy the Hawaiian subject matter called for accentuating greater detail and incisiveness. While the photographs are still enlargements, cropping is rare and only marginal. In contrast to the direct printing on glossy paper preferred by the straight sharp-focus aesthetic, Cassidy chose a textured bromo chloride giving a warm black and rich image tone. It is interesting to note that another Canadian photographer, John Vanderpant, whose work could be seen in Vancouver during the 1920s and thirties, had expressed some very similar aesthetic persuasions. [41] It is possible that Cassidy may have been acquainted with the work of Vanderpant. He certainly would have had the opportunity to observe the artistic activities in Vancouver as a university student. He would also have found the climate of spiritual and philosophical discourse of the era appealing. However, any such connections are speculative and would probably have left no more than a vague imprint on Cassidy's mind.

TORONTO

Shortly after arriving in Toronto, Martin Baldwin, the Curator of the Art Gallery of Toronto, saw Cassidy's photographs. An exhibition was held at the Gallery in December 1938. The reviews were very favourable: the "most fascinating photography exhibition seen in some time,"[42] and a "distinguished exhibition of camera art."[43] Cassidy sequenced the photographs with the intention of establishing specific relationships between images. Reconstruction of the entire series has not been possible, but where a sequence holds between three or more consecutive images (Nos. 22-28), it can easily be seen that Cassidy was not solely taken by the strange beauty of organic growth and captivating natural rhythms. Cassidy linked the isolated forms with strong patterns created by emission of light, playful shadows, and linear systems of tension to state overall texture and symmetry. The images hold an immense clarity of expression, yet they are complex. They manifest a culmination of many-layered universal and symbolic meanings, presenting a special reality whose nature requires spiritual transcendence.[44]

Cassidy's inward search for greater harmony, mystical knowledge, and self-realization led him to find considerable attraction to the teachings of Rudolf Steiner (1861-1925).[45] His philosophy of anthroposophy maintained that by methods of self-discipline, and strengthening of our "soul forces," kinship with the spiritual world could be achieved. Steiner's ideas had their origin in a total view; all plants, for example, are nothing but the materialization of the one, ideal archetypal plant. The notion of Cassidy's Hawaiian plant photographs, beyond their visual representation, is meant to awaken in the viewer the fundamental design of all plants. In Steiner's view:

We have to think of this fundamental design as a living, working idea which cannot be seen by means of our sense organs but which manifests itself in the world of the senses. . . . The archetypal plant is the Proteus who hides himself and manifests himself in all the various forms; and whoever is able truly to imagine this archetypal plant, can somehow invent new plants which do not, or do not yet, exist in the world of the senses.[46]

In Toronto Cassidy set up a studio at 29 Bishop Street. He did a good deal of portrait work and found that he had a special sensitivity for children. His own daughter, Sylvia, was a great source of inspiration and appears consistently throughout his work. In the Hawaiian photograph of 1938 (No. 71) she appears "eye-sweet" and affectionately captured, bringing to mind a sentiment not unlike Eugene Smith's (1918-1978) later but equally affectionate look at his two children in *A Walk to Paradise Garden*. The two informal studies, *Portrait of David* (No. 76) and *Sylvia Sleeping* (No. 77) are remarkable for their tenderness and unsullied repose. The studio portrait studies are more formal and emphasize an economy of style—he normally used only two lights placed on each side on a frontal axis to create integrated illumination. There is little attempt at characterization or conveyance of personality. They possess a measure of quiet intensity, and for the most part they are fine examples of a style that met prevailing requirements. His portrait work was not exclusive to the studio. He frequently took commissions at homes, particularly for children, and he even photographed household pets to churn out a living.[47]

During this period as portrait photographer he began a very personal interpretation of ideas, which he called *Theme of Social Significance*. In this series he adopted a number of different attitudes, allusive and ambiguous on one hand, and straightforward and blatant on the other. Commonplace objects and ordinary spaces are juxtaposed to draw out contrast, such as garbage pails bathed in luminous light—at one time simple and clear as to what they are, but also questioning in their placement (No. 46). The railing of a concrete bridge and telephone wires stringing through space become at once a *Modern Harp* (No. 54) and a mysterious abstraction of shapes. A disorderly, poverty-stricken Ottawa back street is juxtaposed with the highly fashioned architecture of the Parliament Buildings in *Democracy* (No. 45). Titles often offer clues to the ironic content and pictorial logic, and multiple connotations. One can only view this series with psychological resonance and accept their complex equations. In the photograph of his own studio (No. 49), he focussed on a sunflower thrust against the sky while the shabby building is a barely discernible blur. Of the few examples included here, their paradox, irony, and punning suggest Cassidy's disenchantment with man's defilement of nature and the obsolescence of material things surround man. In *Peephole on the Cosmic* (No. 48), the image and implications are almost heavy-handed. These photographs were possibly a reaction to his studio work and a general dissatisfaction at a time when his energies were almost totally consumed by efforts to provide a stable income for the family. The series could also have been a competitive act in response to the highly esteemed photographers who, during the 1930s, had banded together for the purpose of making images to change the world. The Resettlement Administration (later the Farm Security Administration – F.S.A.) in 1935 undertook massive surveys of American life during the Depression. Walker Evans (1903-75) photographed the poverty of the Southern sharecroppers,[48] and the Photo League in New York organized programs on the significance of the documentary to show the true image of the world. *Life* magazine began to publish photo-essays showing the conditions and environments around the world. It would stand to reason that Cassidy would address himself consciously to similar critical issues, but in a more oblique way. His social comment, or social significance, dealt in analogy of principles governing the symbolic, and had very little to do with specific exterior likenesses depicting social crisis and outcry. Cassidy's truer purpose was to make images that would still lay claim to beauty:

Necessity for beauty of form is a principle as nearly without exception as any generalization can be. It must particularly not be relaxed when dealing with ugliness as subject matter. Nor can it be abrogated when dealing with startling and shocking...either with the idea that the compelling interest of subject matter is enough in itself, or because of the difficulty inherent in catching the subject at all...unless they can be presented in as beautifully controlled and formed statement as would be demanded of any other type of subject, they have no right to lay claim to...art.[49]

During this period Cassidy's photographs were accepted into the 48th Toronto Salon of Photography held in 1939, and he exhibited with Toronto Camera Club's spring exhibition.[50]

In an attempt to increase his photography business, Cassidy turned his attention to photographing industrial sites. He chose packing plants, lumberyards, warehouses, grain elevators, and farmsteads. Only negatives remain of these projects, with the exception of an Ontario farm and a grain elevator series on Toronto's waterfront. These subjects posed a new challenge; Cassidy saw the need for a visual approach that would emphasize the elements of the subject's structural organization. Essentially, he investigated the subject in progressive sequences from various viewpoints – from a distance and then close up – to reveal the full range and impact of the site. In the *Grain Elevator Series* (Nos. 64-70) the camera focusses on massive steel beams, creating powerful configurations and tension between black lines and open white spaces. Perspective is distorted to create abstraction.

Eccentric and unusual viewpoints had been explored as early as 1912 in the work of Alvin Langdon Coburn (1882-1966)[51] and consistently by the Bauhaus group and photographers responding to Constructivism.[52] To Cassidy, this new exploration of form was a controlled direction in which he utilized the space bound by the photographic frame to produce a sense of gravity and balance. While there is still a conscientious preference for soft printing, such as in *Men in the Hold* (No. 70), strongly modelled by atmosphere, the overall form and design is a significant departure from his earlier statements.

An even more direct use of the camera image appears again in the series Cassidy produced on an Ontario farm. There is no account or reference to the series other than the fact that the place provided an "impulse to photograph."[53] In these images, elements of the poetic and the concrete appear at the same time with clarity of expression. The farm and its details – barn, haystack, fence, silo, windows, doors – even the ground – are seen as independent images of things that have survived. People as social beings have remained marginal to Cassidy's vision, but in both the *Farmer Leaning on Fence* (No. 61) and the *Man Building Wooden Propellor* (No. 63) they are reminders of man and nature notably connected by industry.

In the farm series one can draw a comparison with Paul Strand's photographs of barns and fences taken in Vermont and Maine during 1944-45.[54] Strand worked with a larger-format camera ($4'' \times 5''$), searching for "the essential character of place and its people."[55] Cassidy's images captured the feeling that the place is being revealed without concealment, that its character is truthful and straight. With the exception of the portrait of the farmer, all of the farm series photos appear full to the edge of the frame. Cassidy saw no need to crop, cut, or otherwise manipulate the images for this series. While his objective would never be to emulate the purist or straight approach to photography, this series emanates a pure simplicity, almost a reductivism, giving credence to the camera's proficiency.

NEW YORK

By the 1940s Cassidy was no longer satisfied with his studio work in Toronto and his marriage was failing. With a strong sense of responsibility to maintain support for his children, he was prompted to seek work in New York. A prior trip had provided contact with art directors, and at *Harper's Bazaar* he met Alexsey Brodovitch, who encouraged him to stay in New York.[56] There is no evidence that Cassidy had photographed studio set-up subjects previously, other than his portrait work. A few negatives exist to indicate that he experimented with photography of glass and metal in daylight situations. It would seem that Cassidy returned to New York with examples of his Hawaiian and Canadian work[57] and was hired by Condé Nast on their merit to photograph for Vogue Studios, specifically as staff photographer for its interior design magazine, *House and Gardens*, in 1941.

Photography at the Studios at first consumed most of Cassidy's time. Other than the occasional portrait study, personal works are rare from this period. Some time later, however, he began an obsessive series of hand studies, of which twenty images culminated into one statement, a work to be seen as a total unit. Cassidy has said that this series was not only a synthesis of what he felt about photography, but in its purest sense it was a wholly metaphysical statement.[58] In looking at the many negatives and the final prints, this series clearly presents an urge to transcend anything else he had previously expressed. The gestures of the hands were not intended as singular studies of the subject reality. To fully understand these images, one has to look for the symbolic meanings in each gesture and the overall relationships they draw attention to. The uninitiated are likely to perceive the gestures as perhaps a

form of sign language–or representation that is visually poetic and rhythmic at intervals, luminous in tonal qualities–but, ultimately, enigmatic. For Cassidy, the hands were a way to express his search for spiritual self-definition. It was a vision meant to translate contemplative and aesthetic concepts into photographic form.

The first sequence of four vertical images calls for spiritual awakening; the images are receptive gestures of unfolding and closing, in which the lotus gesture appears as the essence of life, the whole of existence (Nos. 78.1-78.4). The next four horizontal images speak specifically of yoga philosophy; the beginning of the initial difficulties of facing spirituality and the struggle between desire and ego; in the eighth frame the finger is pointedly in opposition to mind and heart (Nos. 78.5-78.8). The following four gestures speak of yielding, the development into workable form of the spiritual; to be successful, in the spiritual sense, one must be successful with both hands; the fire gesture (frame twelve) indicates that these elements are to be eternal and cannot be extinguished (Nos. 78.9-78.12). Next follows a sequence of gestures for female, union of female and male, and male; the conch-shell-like gesture is a call for attention to the uniting of the soul with (one's chosen) God (Nos. 78.13-78.16). The last sequence shows the prayer gesture; overcoming the last obstacles of desire; and the open-hand gesture of liberation (Nos. 78.17-78.19). At the heart of this philosophy was the concept that materialism separated man from eternal truth. Since everything eventually passes away, all material things are in constant transformation, and therefore illusory. Cassidy's spiritual position was one of seeking enlightenment.[59] The closing image of a reclining nude (No. 78.20) remains extremely personal and, if out of context, it certainly was characteristic of Cassidy to inject a personal impulse that would defy any interpretation. The esoteric meaning of the series is not directly comprehensible, but the images suggest alternative meanings solely by their sheer beauty and eloquence of light, tone, and texture.

The date is not traceable, but the series was probably produced during Cassidy's first years in New York, possibly over a protracted period. He had been to visit Stieglitz at The American Place; Cassidy admired few photographers, but Stieglitz was held in awe.[60] No account exists of what transpired between Stieglitz and Cassidy. Stieglitz, old and ailing, was no longer influential, but he was a mythic presence and a great many photographers sought him out. Although during the 1940s Steiglitz had not exhibited any photography; (the last exhibition he held in 1939 was of the work of Eliot Porter),[61] he still proved to be inspirational. Cassidy very likely identified with – or at least would have been familiar with – Stieglitz's view of the photograph as a metaphor – "an *equivalent* of my most profound life experience, my basic philosophy of life,"[62] – and ultimately his belief that "all art is an equivalent of the artists' most profound experience of life."[63]

While engaging, this highly personal concept of photography was difficult to grasp at the time. More often than not, so inward and imperceptible a world would be met with insensitivity and would be considered remote from the context of the medium's prevailing activities. The beauty of such non-sectarian images of mystical sensibility was carried on by Minor White (1908-1976) who became the leading figure in advocating Stieglitz's concepts through his own work and teachings.[64]

Cassidy took his work with considerable confidence to The Museum of Modern Art. All that is known of that experience is that he was enraged at the museum for their attitude and remained so for the rest of his life.[65] Frequently his deepest emotions were expressed in poetry, an interest from his university days[66]; in a poem titled *Requiem* he pointedly advises not to shed tears for Death, but for the museum.[67] With this rejection, Cassidy felt total estrangement and the desire to redeem his personal photography was no longer actively pursued. Much of his personal vision was encroached upon by the assignments at Condé Nast. It would have been in his character to give himself over with determination to these new challenges. It is ironic that while his attitude was condescending[68] toward commercial work, his visual perception and technical skill in it were extraordinary. In light of Cassidy's distaste for colour, in which he worked predominantly, the quality of his work is even more remarkable. In his essay on colour he wrote:

Contrary to general opinion, the chief difficulties in colour photography are not technical. . . the strictly less technical difficulties are often less than they would be for a black-and-white photograph. Basically the great difficulty lies in trying to work with any freedom

and imagination with that very limitation which appears to the vulgar mind as its greatest asset – its devastating realism.[69]

Colour for Cassidy was stifling and as "an experience without any aesthetic vitality."[70] He felt, however, that it was suitable for magazine "recording of facts" and "for making a record of Junior's developing charms" but "it would never rise above the fleeting values of the topical, the individual, and the literal."[71]

By 1945 Cassidy had all but stopped taking personal photographs. In the *Nude* (No. 79) he returns to a hazier tonal rendering, almost flat and linear in its contours. Yet, for all the concealment of modelling, there is in the figure expanding to full frame a subtle tension and clarity in the deepest end of the tonal scale. *Bedroom Interior*, one of his last images (No. 80) is treated with similar density and stands for an autobiographic event. The somber, melancholic mood reflected his feelings

Figure 4.   Cassidy at work at Condé Nast in the mid-1940s. (© Condé Nast Publications.)

about a deep relationship that had come to an end. [72] In contrast, *Glass Arrangement* (No. 81) and *Girl in White* (No. 82) – are high-keyed in tone. These compositions owe much to elements of design in commerical work – use of strong frontal perspective and a feeling for detached space, fractured by shapes and passages of light. The rather flat luminescence charges the images with a kind of restrained and transparent beauty that only photography can register.

Cassidy continued to photograph elaborate and complex interior decorations, elegant tablesettings, food, flowers, and lifestyles for *House and Garden* until 1955 when he resigned and was never to return to photography again. [73] He gave shape to the rest of his life by pursuing his broad intellectual interests, his love for music and song, poetry and gardening. He persevered through a great many obstacles by singleness of purpose in his spiritual searching but remained somewhat discontented for not having won recognition. In 1958 in a letter to his daughter he wrote:

Obviously it would be quite a wrench to give them [the photographs] up before I die, since they represent one of the most significant phases of my complicated life and are, perhaps, my one relative success, all the more precious to me since it happens to be foreign to the spirit of the age and has therefore passed unnoticed. [74]

Cassidy was in some sense an anachronism. The vision he held of expressing his aesthetic beliefs in the pictorial – the spirit of beauty and truth seen in nature and through abstraction – allowed for little compromise. The renown he achieved with his masterly commercial work was not what Cassidy aspired to, and consequently it only served as a reminder of something not to be upheld as artistic statements. It was useful to meet financial obligations, and when those were met, he saw no further reason to continue. Throughout he had believed in the expressive qualities of the final print, and in the trace of the artist on his work at a time when such traditions about the true relevance of the medium were circumvented by equally strong new ideas. It is only now, when the constant change in the aims of photographers as image-makers are being re-examined comprehensively, that Cassidy, and a great many fine and articulate photographers neglected by time and fashion, are receiving deserved study of their individual contribution and vitality.

NOTES

1. The University of British Columbia Registrar's records.

2. Sylvia Matthew (nee Cassidy) to Shivani Lucki; forwarded to M. Sutnik, December 1980.

3. Matthew to Sutnik, December 1980.

4. For an account of photography between World Wars I and II in Japan, see: John W. Dower, "Ways of Seeing–Ways of Remembering," *A Century of Japanese Photography* (New York: Japan Photographers Association and Pantheon Books, 1980), pp. 14-20.

5. Attilo Colombo, "The Apotheosis of Subjectivity," *Japanese Photography Today and Its Origin* (English ed., London: Institute of Contemporary Arts, 1979), p. 11.

6. Josef Maria Eder, *The History of Photography*, 1945 rev. (New York: Dover Publications, 1978), p. 716.

7. Shinzo Fukuhara, "Japan," *Photograms of the Year 1931: The Annual Review for 1932 of the World's Pictorial Photographic Work*, ed. F.J. Mortimer (London: Iliffe and Sons, 1932), p. 23.

8. Colombo, "The Apotheosis of Subjectivity," *Japanese Photography Today and Its Origin*, p. 11.

9. Dower, "Ways of Seeing–Ways of Remembering," *A Century of Japanese Photography*, p. 16.

10. Raycen Narusawa, "Looking Back Upon the Year," *The Japanese Photographic Annual 1931-1932* (Tokyo and Osaka: The Asahi Shinbun Publishing Company, 1933), p. 1.

11. Erich Hartmann in taped interview with M. Sutnik, New York, August 1980.

12. Matthew to Sutnik, December 1980.

13. E.H. Cassidy, *"Some Theories and a Method,"* Chapter 4: "Tone"; typescript notes, circa 1941-1949, p. 1. Property of J.M. Gitomer.

14. For an examination of the discourse in Britain, see: John Taylor, "Photography in Britain 1900-1920," *Pictorial Photography in Britain 1900-1920* (London: Arts Council of Great Britain in association with The Royal Photographic Society, 1978).

15. Beaumont Newhall, *The History of Photography from 1839 to the Present Day* (New York: The Museum of Modern Art, 1964), p. 77.

16. For a discussion of this issue, see: James Borcoman, "Purism versus Pictorialism: The 135 Years War," *artscanada* 31 (December 1974): 69-82.

17. Eder, *The History of Photography*, p. 715.

18. E. Hartmann in taped interview with M. Sutnik, New York, August, 1980.

19. Isabella Doniselli, "Japan: Tradition and Art," *Japanese Photography Today and Its Origin*, p. 15.

20. Ibid., p. 15.

21. Cassidy, "Some Theories," Chapter 2: "Form," p. 4.

22. Matthew to M. Sutnik, April 1981.

23. E.H. Cassidy, "Aesthetics," typescript undated, p. A/3. Property of J.M. Gitomer.

24. E. Hartmann in taped interview with M. Sutnik, New York, August 1980.

25. Matthew to M. Sutnik, December 1980.

26. Cassidy, "Some Theories," Chapter 4: pp. 4-5.

27. Ibid., Chapter 2: p. 8.

28. Ibid., Chapter 2: p. 2.

29. J.M. Gitomer interview with M. Sutnik, Nevada City, California, July 1980.

30. Cassidy, "Aesthetics," p. A/1.

31. E.H. Cassidy in conversation with M. Sutnik, January 1980. These views also appear in several places throughout his notes on aesthetics.

32. Alice Coates Cassidy, recollection in Matthew to M. Sutnik, December 1980.

33. Newhall, *The History of Photography from 1839 to the Present Day*, p. 114.

34. Ibid., p. 122.

35. Edward Weston, *The Daybooks of Edward Weston: Mexico and California*, ed. Nancy Newall, 2 vols. (Millerton, New York: Aperture, 1973), 2:154.

36. H. Gernsheim, *Creative Photography* (Boston: Boston Book and Art Shop, 1962), p. 172.

37. Cassidy, "Some Theories," Chapter 1: "Choices," p. 2.

38. Ibid., Chapter 3: "Truth," p. 4.

39. Cassidy, "Aesthetics," p. A/4.

40. Cassidy, "Some Theories," Chapter 2: p. 4.

41. For discussion on John Vanderpant, see: Charles C. Hill, *John Vanderpant: Photographs* (Ottawa: The National Gallery of Canada, 1976).

42. "At the Galleries," Toronto *Telegram*, December 21, 1938.

43. *Toronto Globe and Mail*, December 19, 1938.

44. Cassidy in conversation with M. Sutnik, January, 1980.

45. Gitomer interview with M. Sutnik, Nevada City, California, July 1980, and subsequent correspondence, 1981. Cassidy eventually dispelled parts of Steiner's ideas but remained faithful to his teachings related to gardening. Cassidy later formulated his own theories on the topic of biodynamic agriculture.

46. Rudolf Steiner, *The Philosophy of Spiritual Activity*, (West Nyack, New York: Rudolf Steiner Publications, Inc., 1963), p. 14.

47. Matthew via S. Lucki to M. Sutnik, January, 1980.

48. Published as *Let Us Know Praise Famous Men* with James Agee (New York: Houghton Mifflin, 1941).

49. Cassidy, "Some Theories," Chapter 2: p. 3.

50. 48th Toronto Salon of Photography held at the Canadian National Exhibition, 1939. According to the archivist of the Toronto Camera Club, an exhibition was held at Eaton's College Street Salon, Toronto, in the spring of 1939 in which Cassidy exhibited.

51. Newhall, *The History of Photography*, pp. 160-161.

52. For discussion, see: Van Deren Coke, *Photography's Response to Constructivism* (San Francisco: San Francisco Museum of Modern Art, 1980).

53. Gitomer interview with M. Sutnik, Nevada City, California, July 1980.

54. Calvin Tomkins, *Paul Strand: Sixty Years of Photographs* (Millerton, New York: Aperture, 1976), illustrations pp. 48-51.

55. Ibid., p. 24.

56. Matthew to Gitomer, January 1981.

57. A number of photographs taken in Canada bear the stamp "Vogue Studio – Haanel Cassidy." These were stamped for customs purposes to ease the formalities of getting his work to New York.

58. Explained by Cassidy to Gitomer. This is also supported by Cassidy's interest in Eastern philosophies, and specifically the teachings of Paramhansa Yogananda (1897-1952). Also, *Cosmic Consciousness: A Study in the Evolution of the Human Mind*, by Dr. Maurice A. Bucke (1868-1899), was for a time a highly praised philosophical source.

59. I have been assisted by Gitomer and P. Grêhval towards the basic interpretation of the hand gestures.

60. E. Hartmann in taped interview with M. Sutnik, New York, August 1980.

61. Dorothy Norman, *Alfred Stieglitz, An American Seer* (New York: Random House Inc., 1960), p. 237.

62. Ibid., p. 144.

63. Ibid., p. 144.

64. James Baker Hall, "Biographical Essay," *Minor White: Rites and Passages*, (New York, Millerton: Aperture, 1978), pp. 18-19.

65. Related by Cassidy to E. Hartmann and to J. Gitomer; date not recalled.

66. Cassidy preserved a number of his poems over the years. The earliest interest is expressed in a university paper he wrote on mysticism in poetry, largely based on the works of Walt Whitman.

67. Cassidy typescript of poem, circa 1943-44.

68. E. Hartmann in taped interview with M. Sutnik, New York, August 1980.

69. Cassidy, "Colour," undated typescript, p. 2. Property of J.M. Gitomer,

70. The Art Gallery of Ontario, *Bulletin*, November and December 1938.

71. Cassidy, "Colour," p. 3.

72. Related by Cassidy to Gitomer; date not recalled.

73. Erich and Ruth Hartmann in taped interview with M. Sutnik, New York, August 1980.

74. Quoted in Matthew to Gitomer, January 1981, from Cassidy letter to Matthew, December 1958.

No. 1. *Prows*, c. 1933

No. 6. *Temple Morning*, c. 1934-35

No. 5. *Evening Calm*, c. 1934-35

No. 20. *Tea, Orange & Fuji*, c. 1937-38

No. 15. *Just Oiled*, c. 1936-37

No. 13. *(Tea Picker)*, c. 1935-36

No. 10. *Age in the Hills*, c. 1935-36

No. 34. *Plant Form, No. 27*, 1938

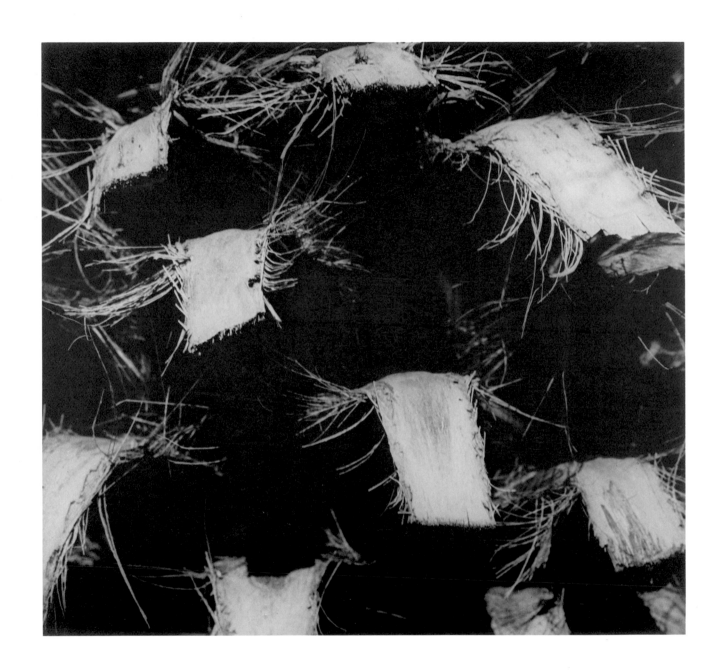

No. 26. *Plant Form, No. 10*, 1938

No. 23. *Plant Form, No. 6*, 1938

No. 38. *Plant Form (Flat Leaf with Shadows)*, 1938

No. 39. *Plant Form – Fugue*, 1938

No. 32. *Plant Form, No. 25*, 1938

No. 37. *Plant Form (Leaves with Circular Protrusion)*, 1938

No. 28. *Plant Form Series*, No. 12, 1938

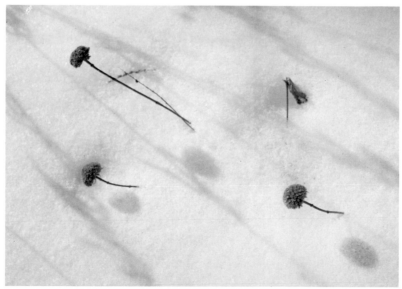

No. 43. *Plant Forms in Snow, No. 3*, 1939

No. 44. *Plant Forms in Snow, No. 4*, 1939

No. 45. *Theme of Social Significance – Democracy*, 1939-40

No. 49. *Theme of Social Significance – My Studio*, 1939-40

No. 54. *Theme of Social Significance – Modern Harp*, 1939-40

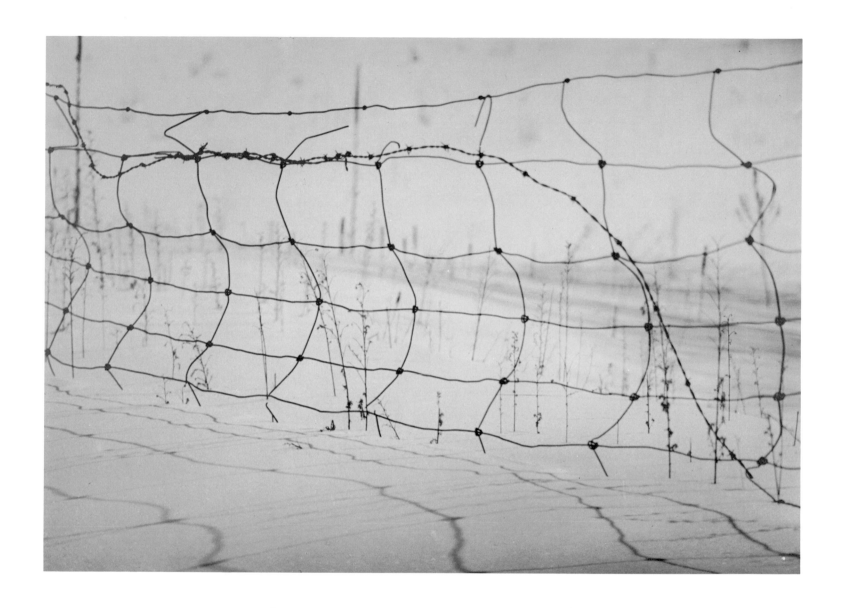

No. 53. *Theme of Social Significance – The Beauties of Nature*, 1939-40

No. 70. *Canadian Industry – Grain Elevator Series (Interior: Man in the Hold)*, 1940

No. 65. *Canadian Industry – Grain Elevator Series (Man on Tower)*, 1940

No. 67. *Canadian Industry – Grain Elevator Series, (Upward View of Loading Conveyors and Towers)*, 1940.

No. 60. *Canadian Farm Series (View of Barn, Silo and Sky)*, 1940

No. 56. *Canadian Farm Series (Side of Barn with Windows)*, 1940

No. 55. *Canadian Farm Series (View of Barns and Haystack)*, 1940

No. 61. *Canadian Farm Series (Farmer Leading on Fence)*, 1940

No. 63. *Canadian Industry – Lumber (Man Building Wooden Propellor)*, 1940

No. 62. *Canadian Industry – Lumber (Cart with Lumber)*, 1940

HAND SEQUENCE

c. 1943-1944

That free and unconditioned consciousness,
which all men briefly experience in certain of their dreams,
is the permanent state of mind of a God-tuned master.
Innocent of all personal motives, and employing the creative
will bestowed on him by the Creator, a Yogi rearranges the
light atoms of the universe to satisfy any
sincere prayer of a devotee.

– Paramhansa Yogananda, *The Law of Miracles*

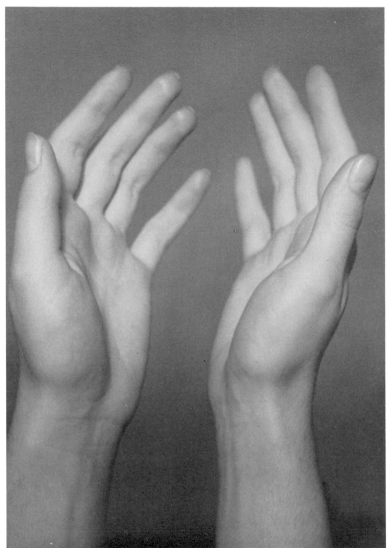

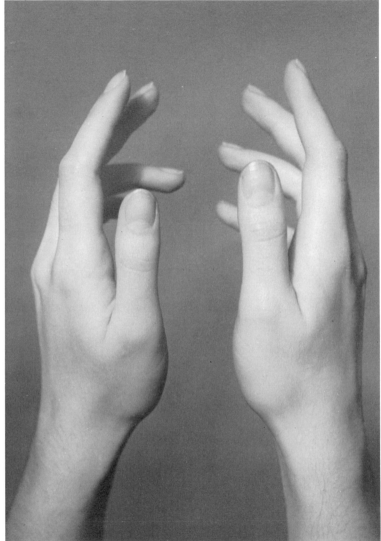

No. 78.1   No. 78.2

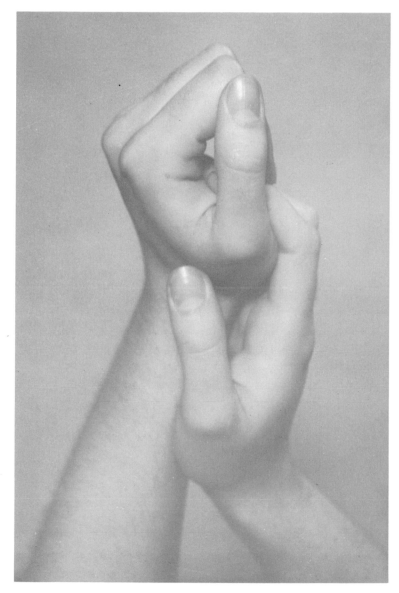

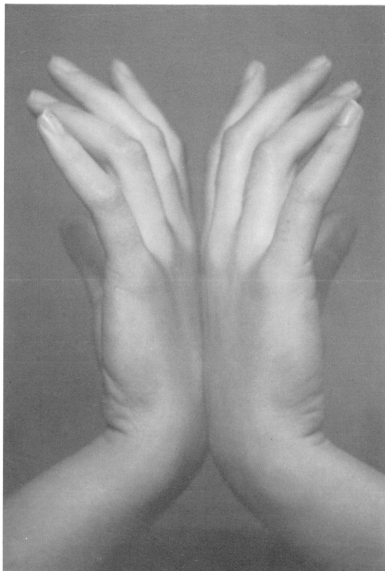

No. 78.3   No. 78.4

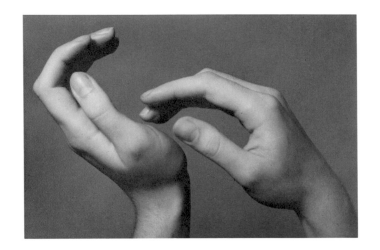

No. 78.5

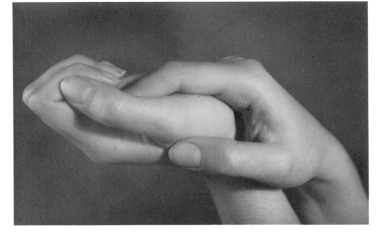

No. 78.6

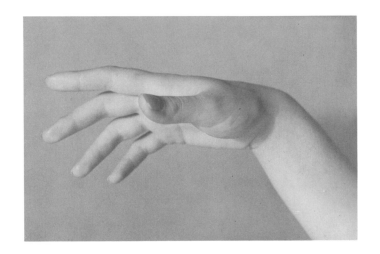

No. 78.9

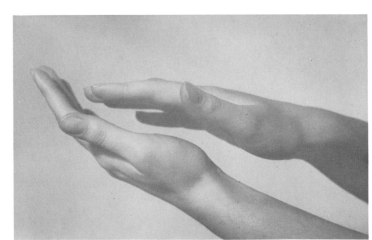

No. 78.10

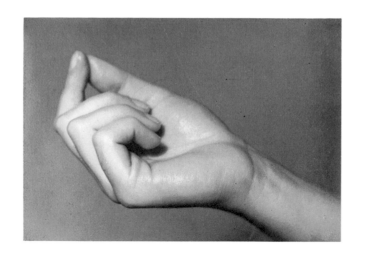

No. 78.7

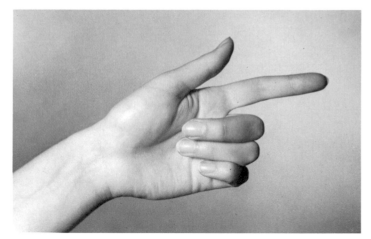

No. 78.8

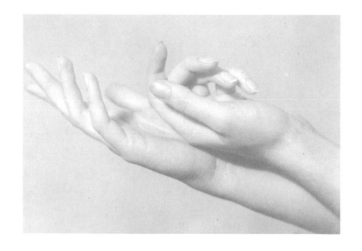

No. 78.11

No. 78.12

No. 78.13

No. 78.15

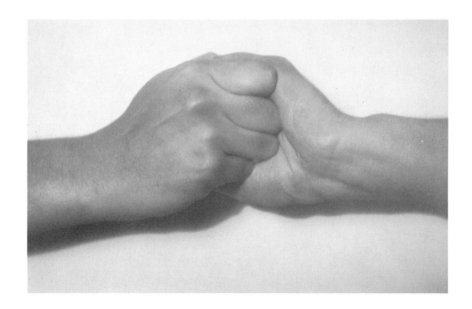

No. 78.14

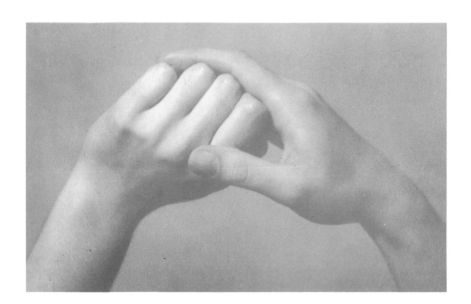

No. 78.16

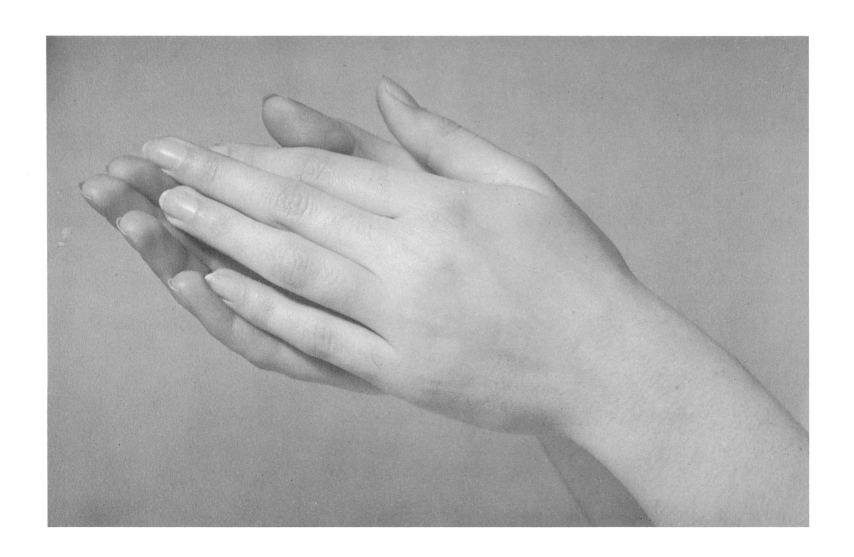

No. 78.17

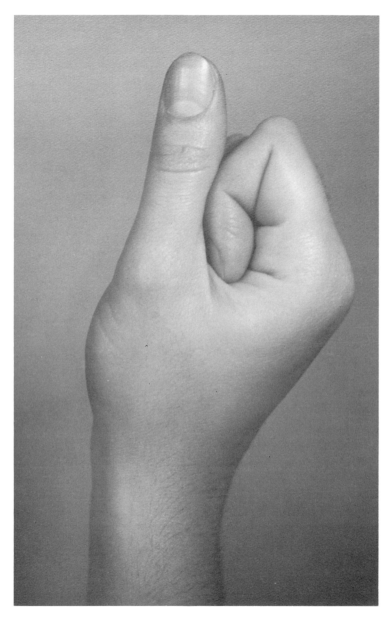

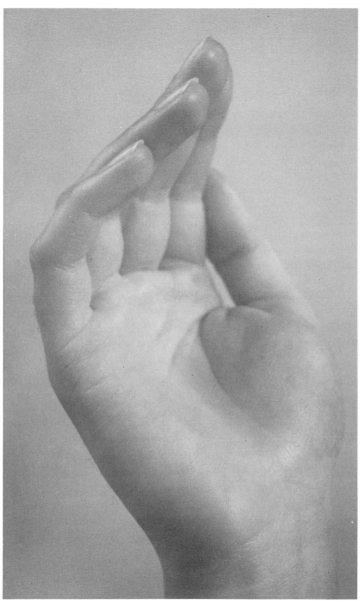

No. 78.18

No. 78.19

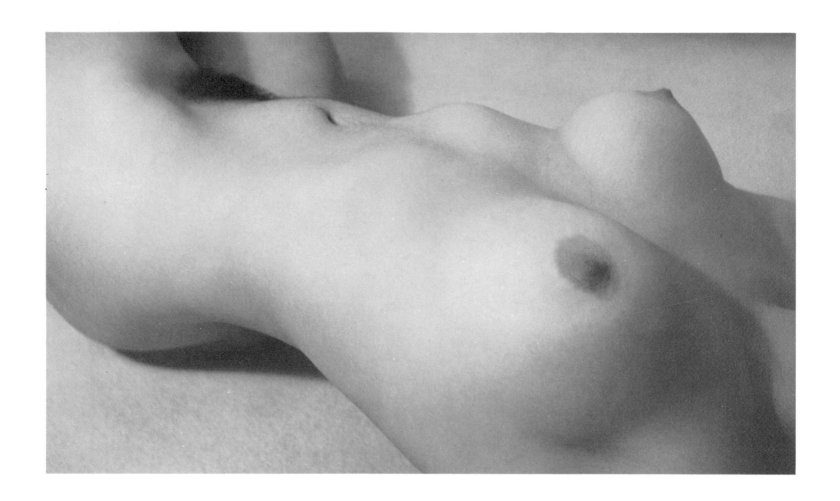

No. 78.20 *Nude*

No. 81. *(Glass Arrangement)*, c. 1945

No. 74. *Portrait of Woman (Sitter Unknown)*, c. 1941-45

No. 72. *Portrait of Hugo Brughauser (Musician)*, 1939

No. 82. *Girl in White (Sylvia)*, c. 1945

No. 76. *Portrait of David*, c. 1942

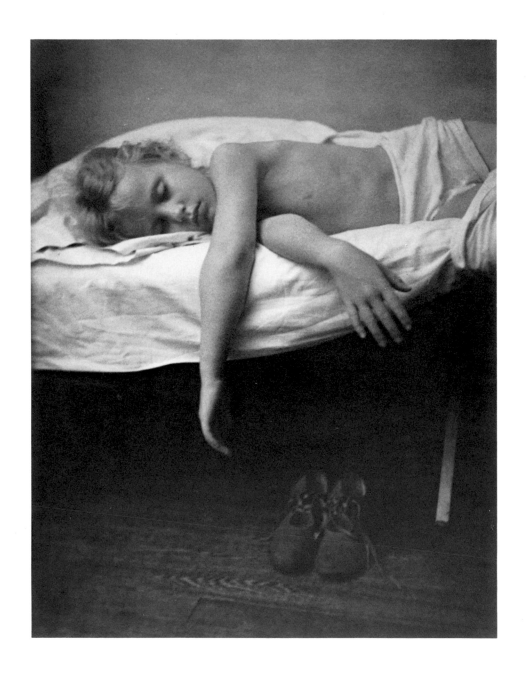

No. 77. *Sylvia Sleeping*, c. 1943

No. 80. *(Bedroom Interior)*, c. 1945

CATALOGUE OF THE EXHIBITION

All works are from the collection of Mr. Joshua M. Gitomer, unless otherwise noted. Titles are given as notated or inscribed by Cassidy. Titles in parentheses have been assigned to aid identification for exhibition purposes. Height precedes width.

1. *Prows*; Japan, c. 1933
   Silver bromide
   28.7 × 23.8 cm
   Initialed in pencil, lrc. on print: EHC
   Inscribed in pencil on reverse: Prows
   In ink on reverse: photographer's copyright stamp

2. *Sunset Satin*; Japan, c. 1933
   Silver bromide
   25.1 × 29.9 cm
   Initialed in pencil, lrc. on print: EHC
   Inscribed in pencil on reverse: Sunset Satin

3. *Japan Mist*; Japan, c. 1934-35
   Silver bromide
   22.6 × 29.9 cm
   Initialed in pencil, llc. on print: EHC
   Inscribed in pencil on reverse: Japan Mist. A view of the Shizuoka plain symbolic of all Japanese rice plains

4. *October Sunrise*; Japan c. 1934-35
   Silver bromide
   22.2 × 29.9 cm
   Inscribed in pencil on reverse: October Sunrise
   In ink on reverse: photographer's copyright stamp
   Collection of Mr. & Mrs. E. Hartmann

5. *Evening Calm*; Japan, c. 1934-35
   Silver bromide
   21.9 × 29.2 cm
   Inscribed in pencil on reverse: Evening Calm
   In ink on reverse: photographer's copyright stamp
   Collection of Mr. & Mrs. E. Hartmann

6. *Temple Morning*; Japan, c. 1934-35
   Silver bromide
   29.9 × 23.5 cm
   Initialed in pencil, lrc. on print: EHC
   Inscribed in pencil on reverse: Temple Morning
   In ink on reverse: photographer's copyright stamp

7. *The Flame Rekindled*; Japan, c. 1934-35
   Silver bromide
   25.1 × 30.2 cm
   Initialed in pencil, llc. on print: EHC
   Inscribed in pencil on reverse: The Flame Rekindled

8. *Wet Weather*; Japan, c. 1934-35
   Silver bromide
   23.5 × 29.5 cm
   Inscribed in pencil on reverse: Wet Weather
   In ink on reverse: photographer's copyright stamp

9. *Paradise Regained*; Japan, c. 1935-36
   Silver bromide
   24.8 × 29.9 cm
   Initialed in pencil, lrc. in print: EHC
   Inscribed in pencil on reverse: Paradise Regained

10. *Age in the Hills*; Japan, c. 1935-36
    Silver bromide
    29.2 × 22.6 cm
    Initialed in pencil, lrc. on print: EHC
    Inscribed in pencil on reverse: Age in the Hills; An Old Country Woman on the Road
    In ink on reverse: photographer's copyright stamp

11. *Ippuku*; Japan, c. 1935-36
    Silver bromide
    20.7 × 24.5 cm
    Initialed in pencil, lrc. on print: EHC
    Inscribed in pencil on reverse: Ippuku. A Japanese farmer rests by his cart on the roadside. "Ippuku" means one "puff" and hence a rest long enough to smoke one pipeful.

12. *Picking Tea in the Land of the Rising Sun*; Japan, c. 1935-36
    Silver bromide
    24.8 × 30.2 cm
    Inscribed in pencil on reverse: Picking Tea in the Land of the Rising Sun
    Collection of Mr. & Mrs. E. Hartmann

13. *(Tea Picker)*; Japan, c. 1935-36
    Silver bromide
    24.5 × 30.2 cm
    Collection of Mr. & Mrs. E. Hartmann

14. *(Viaduct)*; Japan, c. 1935-36
    Silver bromide
    21.7 × 29.9 cm
    Collection of Mr. & Mrs. E. Hartmann

15. *Just Oiled*; Japan, c. 1936-37
    Silver bromide
    24.6 × 36.8 cm

Initialed in pencil, lrc. on print: EHC
Inscribed in pencil on reverse: Just Oiled.
    Japanese umbrellas set out to dry in a
    vacant lot just after they have been oiled.

16. *Pattern in Wood*; Japan, c. 1936-37
    Silver bromide
    20.3 × 29.9 cm
    Inscribed in pencil on reverse: Pattern in Wood
    In ink on reverse: photographer's copyright stamp
    Collection of Mr. & Mrs. E. Hartmann

17. *Fujisan*; Japan, c. 1937-38
    Silver bromide
    29.5 × 24.5 cm
    Inscribed in pencil on reverse: Fujisan.
    Mount Fuji seen from a viewing spot which
    has been famous for centuries. The view is
    usually clouded over soon after seven in the
    morning.

18. *Incense*; Japan, c. 1937-38
    Silver bromide
    28.6 × 24.8 cm
    Inscribed in pencil on reverse: Incense,
    Modern Japan worship to sacred mountain.

19. *Fisherman's View*; Japan, 1937-38
    Silver bromide
    22.9 × 30 cm
    Inscribed in pencil on reverse: Fisherman's
    View. Mount Fuji seen from the shore of
    Shizuoka Bay. (The Japanese, by the way,
    never say Fujiyama, always, Fujisan.)

20. *Tea, Orange & Fuji*; Japan, c. 1937-38
    Silver bromide
    22.6 × 29.5 cm
    Inscribed in pencil on reverse: Tea, Oranges
    and Fuji. A view across the Shizuoka plain
    in May.

21. *Plant Form, No. 1*; Hawaii, 1938
    Chloro bromide
    27.5 × 34.6 cm
    Signed in pencil, lrc. below image: Haanel Cassidy
    Initialed in pencil on reverse: HP1

22. *Plant Form, No. 5 – Armed Neutrality*;
    Hawaii, 1938
    Chloro bromide
    26.7 × 34.4 cm
    Initialed in pencil lrc. on print: EHC signed in

pencil lrc. below print: Haanel Cassidy
Initialed in pencil on reverse: HP5
Inscribed in pencil on reverse: Armed
    Neutrality

23. *Plant Form, No. 6*; Hawaii, 1938
    Chloro bromide
    25.7 × 34.9 cm
    Signed in pencil lrc. below print: Haanel Cassidy
    Inscribed in pencil on reverse: HP6

24. *Plant Form, No. 7*; Hawaii, 1938
    Chloro bromide
    27.0 × 32.2 cm
    Signed in pencil lrc. below print: Haanel Cassidy
    Inscribed in pencil on reverse: HP7

25. *Plant Form, No. 8 – Welcome*; Hawaii, 1938
    Chloro bromide
    27.3 × 33.7 cm
    Signed in pencil lrc. below print: Haanel Cassidy
    Inscribed in pencil lrc. on reverse: HP8
    Inscribed in pencil on reverse: Welcome

26. *Plant Form, No. 10*; Hawaii, 1938
    Chloro bromide
    27.5 × 29.7 cm
    Signed in pencil lrc. below print: Haanel Cassidy
    Inscribed in pencil on reverse: HP10

27. *Plant Form, No. 11*; Hawaii, 1938
    Chloro bromide
    27.5 × 32.7 cm
    Signed in pencil lrc. below print: Haanel Cassidy
    Inscribed in pencil on reverse: HP11

28. *Plant Form, No. 12*; Hawaii, 1938
    Chloro bromide
    34.6 × 23.2 cm
    Signed in pencil lrc. below print: Haanel Cassidy
    Inscribed in pencil lrc. on reverse: HP12

29. *Plant Form No. 14*; Hawaii, 1938
    Chloro bromide
    27.5 × 30.2 cm
    Signed in pencil lrc. below print: Haanel Cassidy
    Inscribed in pencil lrc. on reverse: HP14

30. *Plant Form No. 21*; Hawaii, 1938
    Chloro bromide
    24.9 × 35.1 cm
    Signed in pencil lrc. below print: Haanel Cassidy
    Inscribed in pencil lrc. on reverse: HP21

31. *Plant Form, No. 23*; Hawaii, 1938
    Chloro bromide
    27.6 × 32.1 cm
    Signed in pencil lrc. below print: Haanel Cassidy
    Inscribed in pencil c. on reverse: HP23

32. *Plant Form, No. 25*; Hawaii, 1938
    Chloro bromide
    23.0 × 35.1 cm
    Signed lrc. below print in pencil: Haanel Cassidy
    Inscribed in pencil lrc. on reverse: HP25

33. *Plant Form, No. 26*; Hawaii, 1938
    Chloro bromide
    27.5 × 35.1 cm
    Signed in pencil lrc. below print: Haanel Cassidy
    Inscribed in pencil lrc. on reverse: HP26

34. *Plant Form, No. 27*; Hawaii, 1938
    Chloro bromide
    34.8 × 24.9 cm
    Signed in pencil lrc. below print: Haanel Cassidy
    Inscribed in pencil on reverse: HP27

35. *Plant Form, No. 28*; Hawaii, 1938
    Chloro bromide
    25.1 × 34 cm
    Signed in pencil lrc. below print: Haanel Cassidy
    Inscribed in pencil lrc. on reverse: HP28

36. *Plant Form, (Cactus)*; Hawaii, 1938
    Chloro bromide
    25.1 × 32.5 cm
    Signed in pencil lrc. below print: Haanel Cassidy

37. *Plant Form (Leaves with Circular
    Protrusion)*; Hawaii, 1938
    Chloro bromide
    27.0 × 34.9 cm
    Signed in pencil lrc. below print: Haanel Cassidy

38. *Plant Form (Flat Leaf with Shadows)*;
    Hawaii, 1938
    Chloro bromide
    32.4 × 27.8 cm
    Signed in pencil lrc. below print: Haanel Cassidy

39. *Plant Form – Fugue*; Hawaii, 1938
    Chloro bromide
    35.1 × 27.6 cm
    Signed in pencil lrc. below print: Haanel Cassidy
    Inscribed in pencil uc. on reverse: Fugue

40. *Plant Form – Potentials*; Hawaii, 1938

Chloro bromide
35.1 × 25.7 cm
Signed in pencil lrc. below print: Haanel Cassidy
Inscribed in pencil uc. on reverse: Potentials

41. *Plant Forms in Snow, No. 1*; Canada, 1939
Chloro bromide
25.7 × 35.3 cm
Signed in pencil lr. below print: Haanel Cassidy
Inscribed in pencil on reverse: PFS12-I

42. *Plant Forms in Snow No. 2*; Canada, 1939
Chloro bromide
24.1 × 35.3 cm
Signed in pencil c. below print: Haanel Cassidy
Inscribed in pencil on reverse: PFS5-II

43. *Plant Forms in Snow, No. 3*; Canada, 1939
Chloro bromide
25.4 × 35.1 cm
Signed in pencil lr. below print: Haanel Cassidy
Inscribed in pencil on reverse: PFS5-III

44. *Plant Forms in Snow, No. 4*; Canada, 1939
Chloro bromide
26.2 × 35.3 cm
Signed in pencil lr. below print: Haanel Cassidy
Inscribed on reverse in pencil: PFS4-IV

45. *Theme of Social Significance – Democracy*;
Ottawa, 1939-40
Silver bromide
27.6 × 35.4 cm
Signed in pencil lrc. below print: Haanel Cassidy
Titled in pencil llc. below print: Democracy
Inscribed in pencil ulc. on reverse: SS4

46. *Theme of Social Significance (Two Garbage
Cans and Open Door)*; Toronto or Ottawa,
1939-40
Silver bromide
24.9 × 35.4 cm
Inscribed in pencil ulc. on reverse: SS9

47. *Theme of Social Significance – The
Necessities of Life*; Toronto (?), 1939-40
Silver bromide
25.1 × 35.3 cm
Signed in pencil lr. below print: Haanel Cassidy
Titled in pencil ulc. on reverse: The
Necessities of Life
Inscribed in pencil ulc. on reverse: SS14

48. *Theme of Social Significance – Peephole on
the Cosmic*; Ottawa or Toronto, 1939-40
Silver bromide
26.7 × 35.3 cm
Signed in pencil lr. below print: Haanel Cassidy
Titled in pencil ulc. on reverse: Peephole on
the Cosmic
Inscribed in pencil ulc. on reverse: SS15

49. *Theme of Social Significance – My Studio*;
Toronto, 1939-40
Silver bromide
22.7 × 35.1 cm
Signed in pencil lrc. below print: Haanel Cassidy
Titled in pencil ulc. on reverse: My Studio
Inscribed in pencil ulc. on reverse: SS18

50. *Theme of Social Significance – Adolescence*:
Toronto or Ottawa, 1939-40
Silver bromide
35.1 × 23.7 cm
Signed in pencil llc. below print: Haanel Cassidy
Titled in pencil lrc. below print: Adolescence
Inscribed in pencil ulc. on reverse: SS23

51. *Theme of Social Significance (Rock, Polluted
Water and Branch)*; Toronto or Ottawa,
1939-40
Silver bromide
23.3 × 35.1 cm
Signed in pencil lrc. below print: Haanel Cassidy
Inscribed in pencil ulc. on reverse: SS25

52. *Theme of Social Significance (Weeds
Reflected)*; Toronto or Ottawa, 1939-40
Silver bromide
27.6 × 30 cm
Signed in pencil lrc. below print: Haanel Cassidy
Inscribed in pencil ulc. on reverse: SS26

53. *Theme of Social Significance – The Beauties
of Nature*; Toronto or Ottawa, 1939-40
Silver bromide
24.9 × 34.9 cm
Signed in pencil lrc. below print: Haanel Cassidy
Titled in pencil llc. below print: The Beauties
of Nature
Inscribed in pencil ulc. on reverse: SS27

54. *Theme of Social Significance – Modern Harp*;
Montreal, 1939-40
Silver bromide

26.8 × 35.3 cm
Signed in pencil lrc. below print: Haanel Cassidy
Titled in pencil llc. below print: Modern Harp
Inscribed in pencil ulc. on reverse: SS34(?)

55. *Canadian Farm Series (View of Barns and
Haystack)*; Ontario, 1940
Silver bromide
21.7 × 35.3 cm
Signed in pencil lrc. below print: Haanel Cassidy
Inscribed in pencil ulc. on reverse: CFS3

56. *Canadian Farm Series (Side of Barn with
Windows)*; Ontario, 1940
Silver bromide
25.1 × 35.3 cm
Signed in pencil ll. below print: Haanel Cassidy
Inscribed in pencil ulc. on reverse: CFS5

57. *Canadian Farm Series (Door to Chicken
Coop and Wall)*; Ontario 1940
Silver bromide
26.8 × 34.9 cm
Signed in pencil lrc. below print: Haanel Cassidy
Inscribed in pencil ulc. on reverse: CFS6

58. *Canadian Farm Series (Detail of Fencing)*;
Ontario, 1940
Silver bromide
22.9 × 34.8 cm
Signed in pencil lrc. below print: Haanel Cassidy
Inscribed in pencil urc. on reverse: CFS9

59. *Canadian Farm Series (Side of Barn with
Ladder and Railing)*; Ontario, 1940
Silver bromide
24.8 × 35.3 cm
Signed in pencil lr. below print: Haanel Cassidy
Inscribed in pencil ulc. on reverse: CFS10-3?

60. *Canadian Farm Series (View of Barn, Silo
and Sky)*; Canada, 1940
Silver bromide
24.5 × 35.1 cm
Signed in pencil lrc. below print: Haanel Cassidy
Inscribed in pencil ulc. on reverse: CFS12

61. *Canadian Farm Series (Farmer Leaning on
Fence)*; Ontario, 1940
Silver bromide
27.6 × 35.1 cm
Signed in pencil lrc. below print: Haanel Cassidy
Inscribed in pencil ulc. on reverse: CFS11

62. *Canadian Industry – Lumber (Cart with Lumber)*; Toronto, 1940
Silver bromide
25.7 × 35.1 cm
Stamped on reverse: HAANEL CASSIDY-VOGUE STUDIO (twice)
Inscribed in pencil on reverse: Industry II

63. *Canadian Industry – Lumber (Man Building Wooden Propellor)*; Toronto, 1940
Silver bromide
27.6 × 33.4 cm
Inscribed in pencil lrc. on reverse: C. Industry I

64. *Canadian Industry – Grain Elevator Series (View of Elevators)*, Toronto, 1940
Silver bromide
34.8 × 27 cm

65. *Canadian Industry – Grain Elevator Series (Man on Tower)*; Toronto, 1940
Silver bromide
23.7 × 35.3 cm
Inscribed in pencil urc. on reverse: CM3

66. *Canadian Industry – Grain Elevator Series (Birds on Wires)*; Toronto, 1940
Silver bromide
24.1 × 34.9 cm
Inscribed in pencil urc. on reverse: CM1

67. *Canadian Industry – Grain Elevator Series (Upward View of Loading Conveyors and Towers)*; Toronto, 1940
Silver bromide
24.8 × 34.9 cm

68. *Canadian Industry – Grain Elevator Series (Upward View)*; Toronto, 1940
Silver bromide
23.2 × 35.1 cm

69. *Canadian Industry – Grain Elevator Series (Upward View Showing Ladder)*; Toronto, 1940
Silver bromide
27.3 × 34.3 cm

70. *Canadian Industry – Grain Elevator Series (Interior: Men in the Hold)*; Toronto, 1940
Silver bromide
21.9 × 33.5 cm

71. *Portrait of Sylvia*; Hawaii, 1938
Chloro bromide
30 × 25.1 cm
Initialed in pencil lrc. of print: EHC
Signed in pencil lrc. below print: Haanel Cassidy

72. *Portrait of Hugo Brughauser (Musician)*; Toronto, 1939
Chloro bromide
34.8 × 27 cm
Signed in pencil lrc. below print: Haanel Cassidy

73. *Portrait of Man Reading (Sitter Unknown)*; c. 1941
Silver bromide
27.8 × 32.5 cm
Inscribed in pencil llc. on reverse: IV

74. *Portrait of Woman (Sitter Unknown)*; c. 1941-45
Chloro bromide
31.5 × 24.1 cm
Inscribed in pencil lrc. on reverse: III

75. *Portrait of Woman (Sitter Unknown; Profile)* c. 1941-45
Chloro bromide
35.3 × 23.2 cm
Inscribed in pencil lrc. on reverse: V

76. *Portrait of David*; c. 1942
Silver bromide
23.8 × 35.3 cm
Signed in pencil lrc. below print: Haanel Cassidy

77. *Sylvia Sleeping*; c. 1943
Silver bromide
35.1 × 27.5 cm

78. *Hand Sequence*; New York, c. 1943-44
Chloro bromide
Sequence of 20 prints, 78.1 × 78.20

78.1. *No. 1*
24.6 × 17.6 cm
Inscribed in pencil uc. on reverse: Hands
Inscribed in pencil ulc. on reverse: H1

78.2. *No. 2*
26.5 × 17.5 cm
Inscribed in pencil ulc. on reverse: H 2

78.3. *No. 3*
26.5 × 17.3 cm
Inscribed in pencil ulc. on reverse: H 3

78.4. *No. 4*
26.2 × 17.6 cm
Inscribed in pencil ulc. on reverse: H 4

78.5. *No. 5*
17.2 × 25.3 cm
Inscribed in pencil ulc. on reverse: H 5

78.6. *No. 6*
15.7 × 26.0 cm
Inscribed in pencil ulc. on reverse: H 6

78.7. *No. 7*
17.3 × 24.1 cm
Inscribed in pencil ulc. on reverse: H 7

78.8. *No. 8*
17.3 × 26.0 cm
Inscribed in pencil ulc. on reverse: H 8

78.9. *No. 9*
17.2 × 26.7 cm
Inscribed in pencil ulc. on reverse: H 9

78.10. *No. 10*
17.5 × 25.9 cm
Inscribed in pencil ulc. on reverse: H 10

78.11. *No. 11*
17.5 × 26.8 cm
Inscribed in pencil ulc. on reverse: H11

78.12. *No. 12*
17.6 × 27.0 cm
Inscribed in pencil ulc. on reverse: H12

78.13. *No. 13*
17.5 × 27.5 cm
Inscribed in pencil ulc. on reverse: H13

78.14. *No. 14*
17.6 × 26.4 cm
Inscribed in pencil ulc. on reverse: H14
Inscribed in pencil lrc. on reverse: III

78.15 *No. 15*
17.5 × 22.6 cm
Inscribed in pencil ulc. on reverse: H15

78.16. *No. 16*
17.2 × 27.2 cm
Inscribed in pencil ulc. on reverse: H16

78.17. *No. 17*
17.2 × 26.7 cm
Inscribed in pencil ulc. on reverse: H17

78.18. *No. 18*
26.8 × 17 cm
Inscribed in pencil ulc. on reverse: H18

78.19. *No. 19*
27.0 × 16.0 cm
Inscribed in pencil ulc. on reverse: H19

78.20. *No. 20, (Nude)*
20.7 × 34.6 cm
Inscribed in pencil ulc. on reverse: H20

79. *(Nude)*; New York, c. 1943-44
Silver bromide
34.9 × 27.5 cm

80. *(Bedroom Interior)*; New York, c. 1945
Silver bromide
23.7 × 34.8 cm

81. *(Glass Arrangement)*; New York, c. 1945
Silver bromide
25.4 × 34.6 cm
Signed in pencil lr. below print: Haanel Cassidy

82. *Girl in White (Sylvia)*; New York, c. 1945
Chloro bromide
31.5 × 24.1 cm

1903   Born October 27th, Tokyo, Japan, of Canadian parents. Father, Rev. Francis Albert Cassidy, Methodist minister appointed to the Japan mission in 1886; became the first secretary of Japan Methodist Conference, 1889-93. Mother, Mary B. Haanel, daughter of Dr. Eugene Haanel, prominent professor of modern languages and natural sciences, who held significant university appointments in the United States and Canada, was appointed director of mines of Canada in 1907, and was a charter fellow of The Royal Society of Canada.

1911   Family returns to Canada. Cassidy's father retires to grow fruit in the Okanagan Valley, B.C. Cassidy suffers ill-health and eyesight is impaired. At an early age he is exposed to rigid discipline and scholarly activities by his father.

1920   Cassidy's father dies.

1922   Cassidy awarded Junior Matriculation scholarship; instead takes job with a Vancouver bank to help support mother and two sisters. Failing eyesight is restored by introduction to the Bates System of eye exercises over a prolonged period and remains normal for the next twenty years.

1924   Meets Alice Caroline Coates, his future wife.

1926   Enrolls in a teacher-training course; completed following year.

1928   Enters the University of British Columbia.

1929   Awarded Khaki University and Y.M.C.A. Memorial Fund Scholarship (1928-29).

1930   Graduates with honours in History. Awarded the H.R. MacMillan scholarship. Moves to Tokyo, Japan, with his wife. She holds position as teacher at Jiyu Gakuen Girls' School. Cassidy writes reports to the MacMillan company.

1931   Moves to Yamagata; teaches English at a boys' school. Acquires first camera (plate model). Teaches himself camera and darkroom techniques.

1932   Son David born.

1933   Moves with family to Shizuoka, located few hours outside of Tokyo. Holds position as English teacher with a large secondary boys' school. Pursues photography and acquires the new Exacta camera on the market. Becomes an informal representative for the manufacturer. Obtains portrait commissions from Westerners in Tokyo. Photographs United States Ambassador Grew. Travels throughout the countryside for his personal photography.

1936   Exhibits with Sociediade Fotografica de Zaragosa XII Salon Internationale. Daughter Sylvia born.

1937   Family leaves Japan for Hawaii because of deteriorating political situation.

1938   Exhibits photographs in Honolulu at (?). Photographs major series on native plant life. After six months departs for Toronto, Canada. Gradually acquires portrait commissions, going to homes to photograph children and pets. Opens studio at 29 Bishop Street. Exhibits at The Art Gallery of Toronto in December. Begins to photograph industrial sites.

1939   Exhibits with the 48th Toronto Salon of Photography at the Canadian National Exhibition, and with the Toronto Camera Club Annual Spring exhibition, held at Eaton's College Street Salon.

1941-   Cassidy goes to New York to look for work; prompted by his desire to
44   obtain better-paying assignments and by an interest in another woman, his assistant. He and his wife separate. Moves to New York. Hired by Condé Nast for *House and Garden* and *Vogue* studios. First few years works with a free hand, becomes extremely skilled at photographing glass and silverware. Changes in editorial staff bring about predominantly colour assignments. Becomes a leading photographer of interiors, but does not find this work rewarding. Visits Alfred Stieglitz at An American Place, New York. In his apartment on West 83rd Street

begins to cultivate plants; eventually moves to a house on a large estate in Tarrytown where he takes great interest in growing vegetables and flowers. Writes poetry and essays on photographic aesthetics. Discontinues his personal work.

1945   His family moves to New York, separately. Daughter Sylvia models for many work assignments.

1947   Divorced, family moves to England.

1955   Resigns from Condé Nast. Works freelance through an agency, A.S. Wade on Lexington Ave., New York.

1958   Daughter Sylvia marries. Feels his family responsibilities met and sells all his posessions. Travels to Chile with freighter to farm land given for his use. Arrives after local earthquake and the land is devastated. Attempts to revive it fail and eventually abandons the project.

1960   Returns to the United States and settles in Vista, California. Cultivates a plot of land and makes his livelihood by selling vegetables.

1969-   Moves to Ananda Cooperative Village in northern California, a com-
79   munity founded by Swami Kriyananda in 1967, a disciple of Paramhansa Yogananda (1897-1952), credited with bringing yoga to the West. Cassidy pursues a spiritual life, tends plants, and becomes founder of Ananda Gardens. Develops biodynamic agriculture, teaches composition, voice, and calligraphy to students and devotees of the community. Prepares manuscript for *Organic Growing: The Road to Survival* (to be published by Ananda Publications, 1981/82).

1980   Dies April 16.

GENERAL BIBLIOGRAPHY

Blossfeldt, Karl. *Art Forms in Nature: Examples from the Plant Word*. Intro. Karl Nierendorf, English ed. New York: E. Weyhe, 1929.

Borcoman, James. "Purism versus Pictorialism: The 135 Years War." In *artscanada* 31 (December 1974): 69-82.

Bry, Dorothy. *Alfred Stieglitz: Photographer*. Boston: Museum of Fine Arts, 1965.

Bunnell, Peter C., ed. *A Photographic Vision: Pictorial Photography, 1889-1923*. Salt Lake City, Utah: Peregrine Smith, 1980.

Coke, Van Deren. *Photography's Response to Constructivism*. San Francisco: Museum of Modern Art, 1980.

Dower, John W., Intro. *A Century of Japanese Photography*. New York: Japan Photographers Association and Pantheon Books, 1980.

Eder, Josef Maria. *The History of Photography*, 1945 rev. ed., translated by E. Epstean. New York: Dover Publications Inc., 1978.

Emerson, Peter Henry. *Naturalistic Photography for Students of the Art* (1889). Reprint. New York: Arno Press, 1973.

Fukuhara, Shinzo. "Japan." In *Photograms of the Year 1931: The Annual Review for 1932 of the World's Pictorial Photograhic Work*, edited by F.J. Mortimer. London: Iliffe and Sons Ltd., 1932, p. 23.

Gernsheim, H. *Creative Photography*. Boston: Boston Book and Art Shop, 1962.

Green, Jonathan, ed. *Camera Work: A Critical Anthology*. Millerton, New York: Aperture, 1973.

Hill, Charles C. *John Vanderpant: Photographs*. Ottawa: The National Gallery of Canada, 1976.

Institute of Contemporary Arts, London. *Japanese Photography Today and Its Origin*. Essays by Attilo Colombo, and Isabella Doniselli, English edition, 1979.

Johnston, J. Dudley. "Phases in the Development of Pictorial Photography in Britain and America. In *The Photographic Journal* 63 (December 1923): 568-582.

Maddow, Ben. *Edward Weston: Seventy Photographs*. Millerton, New York: Aperture, 1973.

Millar, Charles. "The Photography of Charles Sheeler." Reprinted in *The Camera Viewed: Writings on 20th Century Photography*, edited by

Pcninak Petruck. New York: Dutton, pp. 111-119.

Narusawa, Raycen. "Looking Back Upon the Year." *The Japanese Photographic Annual, 1931-32*. Tokyo and Osaka: The Asahi Shinbun Publishing Company, 1933, pp. 1-2.

Newhall, Beaumont. *The History of Photography from 1839 to the Present Day*, rev. ed. New York: The Museum of Modern Art, 1964.

Newhall, Beaumont, ed. *Photography: Essays and Images*. New York: The Museum of Modern Art, 1980.

Norman, Dorothy. *Alfred Stieglitz: An American Seer*. Millerton, New York: Aperture and Random House, Inc., 1973.

Renger-Patzsch, Albert. "An Essay Towards the Classification of Photography." In *Untitled 12*. Carmel, California: Friends of Photography, 1977, pp. 16-23.

Renger-Patzsch, Albert. *Die Welt ist Schön*. Munich: Kurt Wolff Verlag, 1928.

Robinson, H.P. *Pictorial Effect in Photography*. London: Piper and Carter, 1869.

Santayana, George. *The Sense of Beauty, Being the Outlines of Aesthetic Theory*. London: Adam and Charles Black, 1896.

Steiner, Rudolf. *The Philosophy of Spiritual Activity*. West Nyack, New York: R. Steiner Publications Inc., 1963.

Steiner, Rudolf. *The Arts and their Mission*. New York: Anthroposophic Press Inc., 1964.

Syberberg, Hans Jürgen. *Fotografie der 30er Jahre eine Anthologie*. Munich: Schirmer/Mosel, 1977.

Tausk, Peter. *Photography in the 20th Century*. London: Focal Press, 1980.

Taylor, John. *Pictorial Photography in Britian 1900-1920*. London: Arts Council of Great Britain in association with The Royal Photographic Society, 1978.

Tomkins, Calvin. *Paul Strand: Sixty Years of Photography*. Millerton, New York: Aperture, 1976.

Weston, Edward. *The Daybooks of Edward Weston, I:Mexico* and *II:California*, edited by Nancy Newhall. Millerton, New York: Aperture, 1973.

White, Minor. *Minor White: Rites and Passages*, biographical essay by James Baker Hall. Millerton, New York: Aperture, 1978.